OZ CLARKE

C000319692

250
BEST
WINES
WINE BUYING
GUIDE 2008

PAVILION

First published in 2007 by Pavilion Books
An imprint of
Anova Books Company Ltd
10 Southcombe Street
London W14 0RA

www.anovabooks.com
www.ozclarke.com

Editor Maggie Ramsay
Design Nichola Smith
Editorial assistant Louisa Veidelis
Tastings and database assistance Sarah Douglas, Catharina Honig, Helen Roylance
DTP Jayne Clementson, Lesley Gilbert

A CIP catalogue for this book is available from the British Library
ISBN-13: 978-1-862-05786-9
ISBN-10: 1-862-05786-9

Printed and bound in France by Qualibris

The information and prices contained in this book were correct to the best of our knowledge when we went to
press. Although every care has been taken in the preparation of this book, neither the publishers nor the editors
can accept any liability for any consequences arising from the use of information contained herein.

Oz Clarke 250 Best Wines: Wine Buying Guide is an annual publication.
We welcome any suggestions you might have for the next edition.

Acknowledgments

We would like to thank all the retailers, agents and individuals who have helped to source wine labels and
bottle photographs.

Please bear in mind that wine is not made in infinite quantities – some of these may well sell out, but the following year's
vintage should then become available. Prices are those which applied in summer 2007. All prices listed are per 750ml bottle
inclusive of VAT, unless otherwise stated. Remember that some retailers only sell by the case – which may be mixed.

Contents

Introduction

'We sell more wine than nappies.' This is the bullish pronouncement of Waitrose's head wine buyer. I found myself wondering, how do you judge what 'more' is, exactly? Number of nappies versus bottles of wine? Volume of wine versus volume of nappy? It's one of those wonderful pronouncements that don't mean anything precise – but you get the gist. It makes more sense than a bewildering but potentially thrilling statement that I read in the *Evening Standard*, which said British wine consumption will grow 3.5 times faster than the world economy by 2010. Can anyone explain that to me? Bullish, yes. **A positive tsunami** of wine must be heading to these shores. But what on earth does it mean?

Well, the Waitrose Pampers versus plonk statement and the bibulous prediction of world economic growth are both pointing in the same direction: our wine market is healthy and it is growing. But which bits of it are growing? If it's only the bottom end, that's pretty dispiriting and makes me wonder what I've been doing all these years. If it's just big brands, which way is **Beachy Head**? Actually, I shouldn't joke, because these so-called brands are indeed racking up increased sales – but more of that later. Or are people perhaps deciding that wine is an interesting enough subject to take a bit of care about, and to spend a bit more money on? There are too many positive signs in the last year or two to say it ain't so.

Waitrose wine sales rose 10% last year, and since they already have the highest average selling price of any supermarket – £5.70 a bottle – **that's not Liebfraumilch** they're selling more of. Now, you might say, oh well, Waitrose is upmarket anyway. Is Tesco upmarket? Well, bits of it clearly are, because they're claiming a 74% increase in sales of bottles over £10 – the average price in their Fine Wine Collection is now £15 a bottle – and you can get some of them in Tesco Metro or Express when you're buying a sandwich or filling up the car. Sainsbury's may have reduced the number of items in their Fine Wine Selection, but that's because small parcels sold out too fast and left irritated customers unable to buy them. Majestic are rolling out another dozen Fine Wine sections and report that their sales are up 25%. So when my taxi driver back from the airport pipes up and says, 'Right, guv, tell me what I should buy for the weekend. Something decent. About 15 quid', I find myself thinking that perhaps as a nation we have got past using wine as a commodity and a significant number of us are prepared to move on to the next phase, to strike out into the confusing but marvellously satisfying world of fine wine.

And nowhere is that more obvious than in the **burgeoning** number of small independent wine businesses that are starting up. *Off Licence News*, the weekly gazette of the drinks retail business, did a survey of the independent wine trade and discovered that 35% of them had started their business since 2000. The modern wine world attracts some pretty **feisty, quirky individuals**. The relentless march of the supermarket giants throughout the 1990s revealed gaps in the market that could be exploited for profit, in particular outside our largest cities. The chance to hand-sell wines, to talk to the customers, to build up a relationship so that they trust your advice – these are things only the most privileged branches of a supermarket can manage. The chance to buy small lots of wine – maybe only a couple of hundred bottles at a time – supermarket buyers wouldn't even deign to taste such a minute parcel. And the chance to specialize. If you're an independent you can decide where your talents lie, **what kind of things fascinate you** and you know you can sell, rather than just trying to be a jack of all trades. And with the massive rise of online trading, you don't even have to have a site where people walk past your door.

And the result of all this? The average price of a bottle of wine sold by the independents is £7.24, against an average price in supermarkets and multiples of £3.59. One third of their wines are sold at between £7 and £8, and over 16% of their sales are in the £10–15 bracket. Not surprisingly, only 5% of their wines are below £5. Quite right too. The only way you can make money at £4.99 and below is by selling large volumes. Leave that to the supermarkets. There is an ever-increasing number of us who are now prepared to pay more for food and drink products which reveal a sense of the people – **real, identifiable people** – who make them, and a sense of the place they come from. Of course, the supermarkets know this, otherwise why would they all be expanding their upmarket shelves? What seems to be happening so far in wine is that the big and the small can co-exist. And it's up to all of us to make sure they do, by buying what we like rather than whatever's cheapest. And ideally we should do it more often. The independents may be thriving, but they still sell only 5% of our take-home wine.

This co-existence question is important in retailing. And it's even more important in the wines themselves. Can small-volume individualistic wines thrive in our market when the 'brands' seem determined to take a bigger and bigger chunk? But what is a 'brand'? Well, frequently it is a drink whose so-called personality is entirely contrived, manufactured. A leading business report this year, talking about brands, said 'Content is not now as important as the image...the importance of country of origin and grape variety is diminishing in favour of brand.' Ugh. The implication here is that substance doesn't matter; packaging, image, promotion and advertising do. **All sizzle, no steak**.

But does a brand have to be bad? Only if it loses all contact with a place of origin and identifiable people. Montana is New Zealand's biggest wine company. Montana is a brand. Yet its wines are recognizably, enjoyably New Zealand and the grape varieties are unmistakable. Concha y Toro is Chile's biggest wine company. Concha y Toro is a brand, and between £5 and £6 their reds and whites are unbeatable value, full of flavour and personality. Yalumba and Peter Lehmann are two large Australian companies. Their wines are brands. Yet they are some of the most **enjoyable and sensibly priced** in the whole of Australia.

But if you look at the top 10 biggest-selling brands in the UK, such excellent producers don't appear. Hardys does. And Gallo. And Blossom Hill, Jacob's Creek, Stowells of Chelsea, Wolf Blass, Kumala, Lindemans. Some of these, like Lindemans and Hardys, used to have a sense of place and personality. Others, like Gallo, Blossom Hill and Kumala, never did; they weren't supposed to. They were created as money-making machines. The marketing was always more important than what went in the bottle. The money was spent on relentless advertising and promoting, not on trying to produce a better wine. It was spent on trying to **grab, grasp, wrestle** a larger slice of market share, regardless of cost. The brand owners would say they are giving the consumer confidence. I would say they are trying to buy, bully, cajole some kind of brand loyalty without ever once considering the true value and quality of the product.

This is a **depressing spectacle** across the whole world of food and drink. It can be extremely difficult to create a big brand and preserve quality because the finance directors and marketing men are obsessed by bottom line and convinced that if they are ingenious enough, if they spend enough, the gullible public won't notice. Some years ago, a famous spirits brand dropped its alcoholic strength and saved itself millions of pounds in tax. I asked what they were going to do with the money saved. They replied they were going to spend it on marketing to persuade consumers the product was just as good as ever. It makes me want to weep.

Of course, you could say that any attempt to sell your product except over the farm gate involves an element of branding, to try to make it stand out in the marketplace. You might well say that the majority of the wine in this guide are brands in some way or other. Rioja Alta is one of Spain's greatest producers – but it *is* a brand. Graham's produces superb port, but it's a brand. Ridgeview is a small, high-quality sparkling wine producer in Sussex. But it is a brand – what else can you call it? So what you *won't* find in this guide are 'brands' which are a monument to 'nowhereness'. What you *will* find are wines with brand names thought up by the owners as ways of **asking for our attention** so that we can taste the fantastic quality of their wines – and remember the name and the label. And you'll also find a fair number of wines that simply state where they come from and who made them. Now, these two can certainly co-exist. And together they can fight the over-promoted, over-discounted dross that will swamp our market unless we stand up to be counted in the name of good wine, real wine, made by real people in real places. When one of the most notorious brand owners was asked why he was suing some tiny producer of a product that was irrelevant to his own and couldn't affect his profitability, he replied 'We don't just want most of the business, we want *all* of the business.' We have been warned.

Wine finder

Index by country

ARGENTINA
Whites
Reds

AUSTRALIA
Whites

Sauvignon Blanc, Philip Shaw no. 19, Orange, New South Wales 37

Sauvignon Blanc-Semillon, Harewood Estate, Denmark, Western Australia 47

Sauvignon Blanc-Semillon, Sandalford, Margaret River, Western Australia 44

Semillon, Tim Adams, Clare Valley, South Australia 23

Semillon, Peter Lehmann, Barossa, South Australia 82

Semillon Reserve, Peter Lehmann, Barossa, South Australia 21

Semillon, Mount Pleasant Elizabeth, McWilliam's, Hunter Valley, New South Wales 42

Viognier-Pinot Gris, Heartland, Langhorne Creek-Limestone Coast, South Australia 48

Reds

Cabernet Sauvignon (Co-op), Coonawarra, South Australia 77

Cabernet Sauvignon Jester, Mitolo, McLaren Vale, South Australia 61

Cabernet Sauvignon, The Willows, Barossa Valley, South Australia 24

Cabernet-Merlot 'The Cracker!', Hope Estate, Western Australia 60

Cabernet-Merlot, Knappstein, South Australia 65

Cabernet-Merlot Reserve, Palandri Estate, Western Australia 73

Cabernet Sauvignon-Merlot, Moda Amarone, Joseph, Primo Estate,

McLaren Vale, South Australia 27

Cabernet Sauvignon-Merlot-Shiraz, Skuttlebutt, Stella Bella, Margaret River, Western Australia 75

Durif, The Boxer, Bill Calabria, Westend Estate, New South Wales 67

Durif, El Gordo, Clare Valley, South Australia 68

Durif, Rutherglen Estates, Victoria 67

Grenache, Bush Vine, Yalumba, Barossa, South Australia 32

Memsie, Water Wheel, Bendigo, Victoria 68

The Partners Reserve, Grove Estate, Hilltops, New South Wales 28

Pillar Box Red, Henry's Drive, Padthaway, South Australia 63

The Red Mullet, Clare Valley, Pikes Vintners, South Australia 74

Saint Macaire, Calabria, Westend Estate, Riverina, New South Wales 69

Shiraz, The Best (Morrisons), Barossa Valley, South Australia 72

Shiraz Reserve, Buckingham Estate, Western Australia 70

Shiraz Reserve, First Flight, South Eastern Australia 92

Shiraz Reserve, Ross Estate, Barossa Valley, South Australia 31

Shiraz, Sanguine Estate, Heathcote, Victoria 38

Shiraz Stonewell, Peter Lehmann, Barossa, South Australia 35

Shiraz, Toa, Coriole Vineyards, McLaren Vale, South Australia 70

Shiraz, Turkey Flat, Barossa Valley, South Australia 29

Shiraz, Wildcard, Peter Lehmann, South Australia 93

Shiraz, The Willows, Barossa Valley, South Australia 25

Shiraz (Yalumba/Marks & Spencer), South Australia 92

Shiraz-Grenache-Mourvèdre, Plexus, John Duval Wines, Barossa Valley, South Australia 31

Shiraz-Viognier, Zonte's Footstep, Langhorne Creek, South Australia 71

Tempranillo, Barossa, Peter Lehmann, South Australia 71

Sweet

Muscat, Campbells, Rutherglen, Victoria 127

Botrytis Riesling, Tamar Ridge, Tasmania 125

Botrytis Riesling-Gewurztraminer, La Magia, Joseph, Primo Estate, South Australia 124

Botrytis Semillon, Keith Tulloch, Hunter Valley, New South Wales 126

Botrytis Semillon, Hermits Hill (De Bortoli/Marks & Spencer), Riverina, New South Wales 125

Sparkling

The Black Queen Sparkling Shiraz, Peter Lehmann, South Australia 115

Jansz Rosé, Yalumba, Tasmania 114
Sparkling Shiraz, Banrock Station,
South Eastern Australia 119

AUSTRIA
White
Grüner Veltliner, Langenloiser Berg-
Vogelsang, Bründlmayer, Kamptal
24
Grüner Veltliner, Obere Steigen,
Huber, Traisental 45
Grüner Veltliner, Smaragd Kollmitz,
Machherndl, Wachau 31
Pink
Zweigelt, Langenloiser Rosé,
Bründlmayer, Kamptal 104
Sweet
Eiswein, Welschriesling, Hölzler,
Weinrieder 124

CHILE
White
Chardonnay, The Society's Chilean
(Concha y Toro), Casablanca Valley
85
Chardonnay Reserva, Viña Porta,
Bío Bío 56
Sauvignon Blanc, The Best
(Morrisons), Curicó Valley 57
Sauvignon Blanc, Floresta, Santa
Rita, Leyda Valley 28
Sauvignon Blanc, Viña Leyda, Leyda
Valley 52
Sauvignon Blanc, Montes, Leyda
Valley 54

Sauvignon Blanc, Secano Estate
(Marks & Spencer), Leyda Valley 51
Pink
Cabernet Sauvignon rosé, San
Medín, Miguel Torres, Curicó Valley
106
Red
Cabernet Sauvignon, Equality/Las
Lomas, Fairtrade, Maule Valley 73
Cabernet Sauvignon-Carignan,
Equality/Las Lomas, Fairtrade,
Maule Valley 79
Cabernet Sauvignon-Carmenère, Old
Vines, Doña Dominga, Casa Silva,
Colchagua Valley 88
Cabernet Sauvignon-Carmenère
Reserva, Viña Porta 76
Carmenère, Atalaya, Viña La Rosa,
Rapel Valley 66
Carmenère, el Grano, Central Valley
75
Carmenère, Viña Leyda, Central
Valley 72
Carmenère, Los Robles Fairtrade,
Curicó Valley 88
Carmenère Reserva, The Best
(Morrisons), Colchagua Valley 76
Merlot, Chilean, Sainsbury's SO
Organic, Central Valley 89
Merlot, Don Cayetano, Colchagua
Valley 77
Merlot, The Society's Chilean
(Concha y Toro), Rapel Valley 90
Petit Verdot-Syrah Reservado,
Tarapacá, Maipo Valley 68

Pinot Noir, Casablanca Valley
(Morandé/Marks & Spencer) 87
Pinot Noir, The Society's Chilean
(Viña Leyda), Leyda Valley 79
Pinot Noir, Cono Sur, Central Valley
78

ENGLAND
Pink
Chapel Down English rosé 104
Sparkling
Bloomsbury Cuvée Merret,
Ridgeview, West Sussex 116

FRANCE
VdP = Vin de Pays

White
Bergerac Sec, Sauvignon Blanc-
Semillon, Domaine des Eyssards,
South-West France 58
Bordeaux, Chateaux's Selection,
Sauvignon-Semillon, Bordeaux
98
Bourgogne Chardonnay, Domaine du
Pavillon, Burgundy 43
Chablis, Burgundy
Domaine Billaud-Simon 26
Domaine Servin 48
Chardonnay, VdP d'Oc, Advocate,
Domaine Saint Hilaire, Languedoc-
Roussillon 53
Chassagne-Montrachet, 1er cru
Morgeot, Domaine Lamy-Pillot,
Burgundy 38

Cheverny, Delaille 56
Corse Sartène, Domaine Saparale, Corsica 47
Coteaux du Languedoc, Picpoul de Pinet, Domaine de Félines, Languedoc-Roussillon 58
Cuvée Pecheur, VdP du Comté Tolosan, South-West France 97
Cuvée de Richard, VdP du Comté Tolosan, South-West France 97
Gros-Manseng-Sauvignon, VdP des Côtes de Gascogne, Alain Brumont, South-West France 53
Les 4 Cépages, VdP des Côtes de Gascogne, Tariquet, Famille Grassa, South-West France 46
Mâcon-Uchizy, Raphaël Sallet/Dom. de l'Arfentière, Burgundy 48
Minervois, Clos du Gravillas, L'inattendu, Languedoc-Roussillon 22
Vie on y est, Domaine Gramenon, Rhône Valley 33
VdP des Coteaux de Murviel, Cépage Rolle, Domaine de Coujan, Languedoc-Roussillon 59
VdP du Gers (Marks & Spencer), South-West France 98
Viognier, La Baume, Languedoc-Roussillon 86

Pink

Costières de Nîmes, Rhône Valley
Château Roubaud 105
Château Guiot 105

Côtes de Provence, Château Saint Baillon, Provence 104
Le Froglet Rosé, VdP d'Oc, Languedoc-Roussillon 106

Red

Beaujolais, Domaine Chatelus 73
Bordeaux
Château Pey La Tour Reserve 62
Lurton La Chapelle 63
Brouilly, Château du Pavé, Beaujolais 62
Carignan, La Différence, VdP des Côtes Catalanes, Languedoc-Roussillon 91
Carignan Old Vines, VdP de l'Aude, Le Sanglier de la Montagne, Caves du Mont Tauch, Languedoc-Roussillon 100
Carignan, VdP des Coteaux de Peyriac, Domaine La Tour Boisée, Languedoc-Roussillon 91
Carignan, VdP des Côtes Catalanes, Empreinte du Temps, Domaine Ferrer-Ribière, Languedoc-Roussillon 35
Chiroubles, Georges Duboeuf 66
Corbières, Caves du Mont Tauch, Languedoc-Roussillon 101
Costières de Nîmes, Château d'Or et de Gueules, Rhône Valley 72
Côtes du Rhône, Rhône Valley
Domaine Gramenon 23
Marks & Spencer 101
Côtes du Ventoux, La Rectorie, Rhône Valley 100

Crozes Hermitage, Rhône Valley
Domaine Yann Chave 60
Domaine Gilles Robin, Cuvée Albéric Bouvet 26
Domaine Gilles Robin, Papillon 61
Cuvée de Richard, VdP de l'Aude, Languedoc-Roussillon 101
Grenache Fruits of France, VdP d'Oc, Languedoc-Roussillon 99
Minervois la Livinière, La Cantilène, Chateau Sainte-Eulalie, Languedoc-Roussillon 65
Moulin-à-Vent, Château de Chénas, Beaujolais 29
Saumur Rouge, Les Nivières, Loire Valley 87
St-Nicolas de Bourgueil, Frederic Mabileau, Loire Valley 27
Syrah, VdP d'Oc, Camplazens, Château Camplazens, Languedoc-Roussillon 76
Vacqueyras, Rhône Valley
Domaine le Sang des Cailloux 39
Domaine Bastides d'Eole 64
VdP de l'Ardèche Gamay, Rhône Valley 99

Sparkling

Cabernet Rosé Brut, Ackerman, Loire Valley 119
Champagne
Blanc de Blancs (Waitrose) 114
Deutz 117
Fleury 118
Charles Heidsieck 117
Oudinot 116, 118

Premier Cru (Union Champagne/Tesco) 119
The Wine Society's Private Cuvée (Alfred Gratien) 117
Sweet
Monbazillac, Domaine du Haut-Rauly, South-West France 126

GEORGIA
White
Mtsvane, Tamada 53
Red
Saperavi Reserve, Tamada 65

GREECE
White
Hatzidakis, Santorini 45

HUNGARY
White
Matra Springs, Gyöngyös 98
Pinot Grigio (Hilltop Neszmély/Marks & Spencer) 96
Riesling, Budai, Nyakas 59

ITALY
White
Blanc de Morgex et de la Salle, Vini Estremi, Valle d'Aosta 44
Fiano-Greco, A Mano, Puglia 56
Soave, La Rocca, Pieropan 30
Verdicchio dei Castelli di Jesi Classico, Moncaro 96

Reds
Amarone della Valpolicella, Ca' La Bionda 22
Barbera d'Asti Superiore, Trinchero 62
Montepulciano d'Abruzzo, Casale Vecchio 64
Nerello Mascalese, Sicily 90
Terrano, Carso, Zidarich, Friuli-Venezia Giulia 36
Trinacria Rosso, Sicily 100
Valpolicella Classico, Allegrini 34
Sparkling
Prosecco
Vincenzo Toffoli 120
Vigna Del Cuc, Case Bianche, Martino Zanetti, Veneto 120

NEW ZEALAND
White
Chardonnay, Explorers Vineyard 58
Chardonnay, Fairleigh Estate, Marlborough 52
Chardonnay, Stoneleigh, Marlborough 32
Riesling, Danny Schuster, Waipara 54
Sauvignon Blanc, Dashwood, Marlborough 55
Sauvignon Blanc, Explorers Vineyard 55
Red
Pinot Noir, Hatter's Hill, Delta Vineyard, Marlborough 30
Pinot Noir, Stoneleigh, Marlborough 60

Syrah, Villa Maria Cellar Selection, Hawkes Bay 20
Sparkling
Bluff Hill (Marks & Spencer) 116
Pelorus, Cloudy Bay 114

PORTUGAL
White
Ribatejo, Portal da Águia 85
Red
Douro, Quinta do Crasto (Sainsbury's) 74
Quinta de Bons-Ventos, Casa Santos Lima, Estremadura 90
Touriga Nacional, Tesco Finest, Quinta da Fonte Bela, Estremadura 78
Port
10-year-old Tawny Port, The Society's Exhibition 135
10-year-old Tawny Port, Taylor's 136
10-year-old Tawny Port, Warres Otima 136
1995 Vintage Port, Quinta da Roeda, Croft 133
1998 Vintage Port, Taylor's Quinta de Vargellas 133
2000 Vintage Port, Quinta do Crasto (Sainsbury's) 134
Crusted Port, Tanners (Churchill Graham) 134
LBV Port, The Society's (Symington Family Estates) 135
Reserve Port, Terra Prima, Fonseca 134

ROMANIA
White
Pinot Grigio, Recas 97

SOUTH AFRICA
White
Chardonnay, Rustenberg,
  Stellenbosch 37
Sauvignon Blanc, Excelsior Estate,
  Robertson 83
Sauvignon Blanc, M'Hudi, Elgin 50
Sauvignon Blanc, Ormonde Cellars,
  Darling 55
Viognier, Brampton (Rustenberg) 51
Pink
Slowine Rosé 105
Red
Pinotage, Diemersfontein, Wellington
  69
Pinotage, Houdamond, Bellevue
  Estate, Stellenbosch 69
Syrah, Porcupine Ridge
  (Boekenhoutskloof) 74
Syrah, TMV, Swartland 33

SPAIN
White
Albariño, Rías Baíxas, Galicia
  Sainsbury's 57
  Val do Sosego 52
La Basca Uvas Blancas (Marks &
  Spencer), Castilla y León 83
Chardonnay, Hacienda el Espino
  1707, Almansa, Castilla-La
  Mancha 49

Rueda, Casa del Sol, Sauvignon
  Blanc-Verdejo, Castilla y León 84
Pink
Marqués de Rojas, Bodegas
  Piqueras, Almansa, Castilla-La
  Mancha 106
Navarra, Malumbres 107
Navarra, Torre Beratxa 107
Ribera del Duero , El Quintanal,
  Castilla y León 105
Rioja, Gran Familia, Bodegas Castillo
  de Fuenmayor 106
Tempranillo, Tierra Sana, La Mancha
  107
Utiel-Requena, Viña Decana, Valencia
  107
Red
Conca de Barberà, Cabernet
  Sauvignon-Merlot, Marqués del
  Costal, Cataluña 67
Costers del Segre, Raimat Abadia,
  Cataluña 77
Garnacha Tinto, Navarra 87
Ribera del Duero, Dominio de
  Nogara, Bodegas Valtravieso,
  Castilla y León 75
Rioja Reserva Elegia, Torre de
  Oña/Rioja Alta (Sainsbury's) 64
Tempranillo-Syrah, Palacio del
  Marqués (Marks & Spencer),
  Castilla-La Mancha 87
Toro, Finca Sobreño, Castilla y León
  93
Syrah, Finca Antigua, La Mancha
  78

Sparkling
Cava Brut, Pinot Noir, Codorníu 120
Cava Brut, Vineyard X, Covides 121
Cava Reserva Brut Rosado, Palau
  Gazo 121
Vintage Cava Brut
  (Codorníu/Sainsbury's) 121
Fortified
Amontillado Sherry (Emilio
  Lustau/Sainsbury's) 131
Amontillado Viejo, Delgado Zuleta
  132
La Copita Fino 131
Don PX Gran Reserva, Montilla-
  Moriles 127
Manzanilla Extra Dry Sherry, Marks &
  Spencer (Williams & Humbert) 130
Manzanilla Pale Dry Sherry,
  Sainsbury's (Emilio Lustau) 130
Manzanilla, Tanners Mariscal,
  Dolores Bustillo Delgado 130
East India Solera, Emilio Lustau
  131
Rich Cream Sherry, Marks & Spencer
  (Williams & Humbert) 132
Solera 1847, Sweet Cream Sherry,
  González Byass 132

USA
Red
Shiraz Reserve, The Boulders,
  California 92
Zinfandel, The Best (Morrisons),
  California 79

TOP
250

**TOP
40**

This is a magnificent array of the thrilling flavours the world of wine offers. I've chosen them because they sparkle with personality. This may be the looming gastronomic shadow of a vinous Big Beast, or it may be their delicacy, freshness and subtlety, but each wine has given me enormous pleasure this year, and cheered me up when I began to convince myself that our exciting wine world was destined to be swallowed up by the mighty international conglomerates and their allies the retail giants, whose bloodletting discounting policies leave so many producers wondering if it's worth carrying on. Whether they *can* carry on. Well, the producers here – large and small, famous or unknown – flourish by pledging themselves to produce the best wine they can. The two most successful countries are Australia and France. And if anyone fears that these countries' wines are becoming homogenized – check out these winners. Every one unique and memorable.

This chapter lists my favourite wines of the year, both red and white:
 = red wine ♦ = white wine

1 2005 Syrah, Villa Maria Cellar Selection, Hawkes Bay, New Zealand, 13.5% ABV

♦ Threshers, £14.99 (3 for 2, £9.99)

You'll never have tasted anything like this. I visited Hawkes Bay in New Zealand's North Island this year, and most of the land is not only unsuitable for Syrah, it's unsuited for grapes of any kind. But there's one slab, one chunk, one unlovely plot of this sparse land that used to be famous (well, locally) as the site of the speedway track, the town dump and the army ranges. Why was no one farming it? Gravel. Pure gravel. Gravel so pure nothing would grow and even the plentiful Hawkes Bay rains drained straight through. But these gravels, known as the Gimblett Gravels, are also warm – much warmer than the thick fertile clays that clog the rest of the region. And someone had a brainwave. The soils are so free-draining that the rain doesn't matter. And they're so warm that previously unthought-of warm-climate grapes might grow there. But surely not Syrah – the denizen of France's Rhône Valley and, as Shiraz, the brawny beast of Australia? A band of bravehearts gave Syrah a go – and it works, brilliantly. It's not like any Syrah or Shiraz you've ever tasted before. It's a totally new flavour and I'm excited and amazed it's already hit our high streets. It's a fresh, purpley red. The smell will shock you – white pepper, lovage, curry plant, angostura, violet stems – what is this? So taste it. All of those rare, shocking, red wine tastes are there, but the texture is supremely gentle – bone-dry, duck-down gentle – and the fruit is also bone dry but blazing with blackberry, blackcurrant and mulberry, speckled with graphite dust and wrapped in cream. And it's bone, bone dry.

2 2000 Semillon Reserve, Peter Lehmann, Barossa Valley, South Australia, 11.5% ABV
♦ Portland, Vin du Van, Noel Young, £10.99

Australian whites don't get much better than this. Or more traditional. This isn't some oak-soaked monster begging for high 90s on the 100-point scale – this is totally un-oaked, it's low in alcohol and it couldn't care what mark it got in the tasting tournaments – this is how it was always made and nothing's gonna change. Thank God, because this is a great original. It's a big wine, deep, but not heavy. It's got a wonderful weight of custard cream and leather, citrus lime zest and a splash of blood orange juice – and is there a drop of petrol there too? Maybe not, it's just that the lime zest isn't so much a thread as a torrent racing through the wine, gathering up the custard cream and hazelnut richness as it hurtles on, but every mouthful you grab is the real deal. Are you ready?

3 2005 Chardonnay, Diamond Valley, Yarra Valley, Victoria, Australia, 14% ABV
♦ Oz Wines, £10.99

For all of us who've taken one too many mouthfuls of Australian Chardonnay and said yuk, never again – this is the wine for you. Did the terms elegance, subtlety, Burgundian restraint even cross your mind as you spat out the typical blowsy overoaked Aussie Chardie? And did you think, damn, I really liked Down-Under Chardonnays – once? Here's your salvation. From a sylvan retreat high in the hills above the Yarra Valley, so close to Melbourne's metropolis on the map, yet so far away on these quiet hillsides where the kangaroos and bellbirds might

interrupt your musings, but nothing else will, they grow heavenly Chardonnay, as it should be grown. It's soft and mellow, there's a soothing and not at all intrusive clove and nutmeg spice when you smell it, but as you take a mouthful the spice melts into a soft rounded world of white peach flesh and this then melts into a world of oatmeal, honey and nuts. Which is sort of … fine Burgundy, isn't it? Sure. At twice the price of this.

4 2000 Amarone della Valpolicella, Ca' La Bionda,
    Veneto, Italy, 15.5% ABV
    ◆ Bat & Bottle, £25.00

It's not really fair to throw an Amarone into the middle of a tasting.
Amarone is such a bizarre, severe, maverick style of wine it can
pervert the pure conventional flavours that may surround it. But I
say, bad luck on them, because I wouldn't want to miss this for
anything. When you see Amarone on the label, don't expect the
expected. And don't expect this marvellous maverick of a wine to show its glittering character when young.
Amarone needs five years, would prefer ten and is delighted with 15. So 2000 – seven years old – is a fair
compromise, showing us its character, but I promise, hold on to this wine and it'll be transformed, richer,
sweeter yet more sour, in five to ten years' time. For now? A fabulous cacophony of ripe apple peel and
lightly baked apple pie with sweet cherry flesh and sour cherry skin. There's a dryness of stones – cold,
grey – and it's necessary, because the fruit reasserts itself with a flurry of baked figs and cherries, syrup
and the scented smoke of fruit toasted on a grill that moments ago had served up beef.

5 2005 Minervois, L'inattendu, Clos du Gravillas, Languedoc-Roussillon, France, 14% ABV
    ◆ les Caves de Pyrene, £13.62

This shows why you must never grub up old vines. These vines were
planted in 1911, and the name – L'inattendu – what do you think? The
neglected, the un-waited for, the unexpected? Whatever. No one had
loved, cared for, caressed these vines for generations until an unlikely
couple from Narbonne and Kentucky (yes, Kentucky, America) bought
the plot and thought – uproot or cherish? They chose cherish. This
white is made from the rare, sort of mutant grape, the half-white half-

red Grenache Gris. The wine is lush and unnerving but the lushness is what matters – rich, buttered brazils and hazelnut cream. Fatness everywhere. Fat apple, fat caramel, fat brazil nut – and yet lovely acidity, lovely balance, strange and rare.

6 2005 Semillon, Tim Adams, Clare Valley, South Australia, 13% ABV
   ◆ Tesco, £8.99

Tim Adams is a wonderful guy, a remarkable guy, because he seems able to reconcile two opposites. Every year he makes a Semillon that amazes you with its consistency – consistency of supreme quality and utterly fair price. Yet every year it tastes completely different. There's the paradox, there's the genius. A vertical tasting of all the Semillon he has made would be one of the great wine tastings. Forget white Burgundy or Sauternes. Taste 20 years of Adams' Semillon! So what's this one like? Big. Rich. Exotic. A heady mix of nutmeg, ginger, custard, leather and nectarine to start. Just to start? Yes, but the thing about Tim's wines is they evolve – in your mouth, not just in the bottle – and so you'll find the crystallized sugar of Bath buns, smoky toasted cashew nuts, lemon zest, beeswax fatness and the homely warmth of a baked peach tart. In which order these flavours come depends on you – they're all there.

7 2006 Côtes du Rhône, Sierra du Sud, Domaine Gramenon, Rhône Valley, France, 14% ABV
   ◆ les Caves de Pyrene, £12.28

Why is this stuff so good? Maybe because it's grown way north of the mainstream Côtes du Rhône in a tiny village called Montbrison, tucked up into the eastern hills miles away from tourism and commerce, so you don't get endless interruptions just when you don't need them. And Michèle Laurent makes good use of this isolation by doing everything by hand: pruning, harvesting, making the wine, even bottling it by hand. This wonderfully old-style passion shows in the wine. This is 100% Syrah from what Michèle might say are adolescent vines – only 30 years old – but the intense personal care in vinegrowing and winemaking creates a remarkable red – an astonishing scent of parsley and sandalwood and soap, swirled with smoke and tumbled about with a great flood of ripe blackberry and damson. It's a brilliant, unexpected mishmash – and it works.

8 2004 Cabernet Sauvignon, The Willows Vineyard, Barossa Valley, South Australia, 14.5% ABV

♦ Oz Wines, £12.99

You just never know where you are with The Willows. Well, you always know where you are in that The Willows is always going to supply some of the most joyously lush and pleasurable wines in your year's drinking. But will it be the Shiraz, the Cabernet or the Semillon? This year, as usual, they're all good, but the Cabernet just leads the pack. It manages to be fantastically ripe yet never overripe, balanced but profoundly rich and fruity, loads of everything, but never too much, a thrilling dry maelstrom of sweet blackcurrant – real throat pastille stuff – scented with peppermint and eucalyptus leaf. Good? Sure, but there's also an undertow of fern and forest floor decay which only enhances the brilliance of the wine.

9 2005 Grüner Veltliner, Langenloiser Berg-Vogelsang, Bründlmayer, Kamptal, Austria, 12.5% ABV

♦ Waitrose, £12.99

If I had to say which white wine grape in Europe has consistently given me the most pleasure this year – and probably last year too – I think I'd plump for Grüner Veltliner. And before you say – who, what? – I know it doesn't sound familiar, and the name of this wine is just too Germanic for words, but it isn't German, it's nothing like German wine in flavour or style – the Germans don't even grow the grape! This is Austria at its finest. From a horrible nadir about 20 years ago when a couple of villains were discovered adding antifreeze to some of their wines, Austria has quietly set to re-inventing itself, and now makes some of the most exciting whites in the world, and some pretty good reds and pinks too. But, of course, for us Brits, most of whom take to foreign languages like a midge to fly spray, the German words and interminable names are a massive turn-off. So, just let me say this. Bründlmayer is a great winemaker and it's your loss if you don't try this nectar. And this Grüner Veltliner is a star wine, quite unlike any of the other whites you'll be drinking. For a start it's got an amazing smell of radish, celery, white pepper and kid glove leather. If this sounds sharp, have a taste and you'll discover a magically soft wine – yet crisp and green – all those peppery, radishy flavours somehow swathed in goldengage and soft syrup. And it's dry. And remember, Bründlmayer is a big guy and he really wouldn't like it if you thought he was German.

10   2002 Shiraz, The Willows Vineyard, Barossa Valley, South Australia, 14.5% ABV
   ♦ Oz Wines, £10.99

I don't know how the guys at The Willows do it. The Barossa is going through a bit of an OTT phase at the moment with its Shiraz – too many expensive wines tasting like raisin syrup. But at The Willows, the price stays the same, the alcohol stays high, the wine is as ripe as you could wish but wonderfully fresh. You can drink this in draughts on a cold winter's eve, not just sip it and secretly want to dilute it with mineral water. It's now quite mature, it's lost a little of its braggart youth, and it's brimming with the delightful flavours of chocolate, blueberry, eucalyptus and blackcurrant, all at ease with each other, melded, married and wrapped in a dry black cocoon of liquorice that actually cleanses your palate as you swallow – *most* unusual for a high-octane Aussie Shiraz.

11   2005 Crozes Hermitage, Cuvée Albéric Bouvet, Gilles Robin, Rhône Valley, France, 13.5% ABV

♦ Great Western Wine, £13.95

Crozes Hermitage for generations has been described as a kind of minor Hermitage. Well, it's true that Hermitage does occupy all the traditionally best slopes on its great hill tumbling down to the banks of the Rhône. But many growers in Crozes have now stopped trying to ape the beefy, long-lived intensity of Hermitage and thought – is there a better style, our own Crozes style? Yes, there is. And this is a beautiful example of high-quality modern Crozes, bearing no resemblance to beetle-browed Hermitage. This is pure pleasure, creamy in texture, absolutely bubbling with ripe blackberry and loganberry fruit with a few hillside herbs gamely swimming around in the delightful broth – and an imp sits at the edge wafting perfumed violets into the air.

12   2005 Chablis, Domaine Billaud-Simon, Burgundy, France, 12% ABV

♦ H & H Bancroft, The Wine Society and other independent retailers, £9.95

The label states, 'Our purpose: to offer an ethereal, crystalline Chablis emotion…' What a delightful idea. And how well they've achieved it. Too many modern Chablis are tasting positively creamy in an unwelcome move towards disowning their birthright. I like ripe Chablis, sure, but this is as ripe as it needs to be and it's

only 12 per cent alcohol. Push this up to 13.5 by minimizing the yield and leaving what grapes are left to overripen into the autumn, and you lose the whole point of Chablis. As it is, this is very pure, ripe but delicate, intense yet ethereal. Cool white apple flesh and mellow lemon acidity softened just a little by brioche yeast then brought back into line with a finely judged – yes, 'crystalline' – minerality. Beautifully balanced classic Chablis.

13 2004 Cabernet Sauvignon-Merlot, Moda Amarone, Joseph, Primo Estate, McLaren Vale, South Australia, 14.5% ABV

♦ Philglas & Swiggot, £22.99

Joe Grilli is one of Australia's great innovators. He could have decided to make a high-quality Cabernet-Merlot blend in the classic Bordeaux style. But no. He says he doesn't want to make a slightly better Cabernet than someone else. He wants to dazzle people. He says he believes the role of small wineries is to explore the unconventional, so he makes his Cabernet-Merlot as though he were making an Amarone in Valpolicella in Italy! He partially dries the grapes before fermenting them. This gives the wine a fantastic richness but also a thrilling black chocolate bitterness that gnashes its teeth at the dense, ripe, black plum and black cherry fruit and, in time, five years maybe, will blend into a bittersweet beauty rarely equalled in a red wine. This is still very young – magnificent but unresolved. By all means drink it now for its pent-up power and grandeur, or buy it and leave it, and finally have one of the great red wine experiences of your life.

14 2005 St-Nicolas de Bourgueil, 'Les Rouillères', Frederic Mabileau, Loire Valley, France, 13% ABV

♦ Waitrose, £9.05

This is quite simply one of the most delightful – and best value – red wines that is produced in the whole of France. St-Nicolas is a village in the Loire Valley that specializes in Cabernet Franc, and makes a sublime red from it that seems to sing with the boundless optimism of spring and early summer. And this isn't light – it's got a concentration of fully ripe loganberry and raspberry that seamlessly blends with a cleansing, purifying, pale pebble dryness, and the whole experience is truly fruit-driven yet marvellously harnessed by the dryness of summer dust. 2005 made supreme reds in the Loire. Indulge in them while they last.

15 2004 The Partners Reserve (Sangiovese, Nebbiolo, Petit Verdot, Barbera), Grove Estate Wines, Hilltops, New South Wales, Australia, 14.5% ABV

♦ Oz Wines, £12.99

I love it when the Aussies really start to show the world what they're made of by innovating, imagining, taking the risks of brickbats or plaudits. These guys are in a little-known 'cool' – well, cool for New South Wales – place upon the high ground near the nation's capital, Canberra. Growing Italian varietals is *not* the way to make a quick buck, and blending Bordeaux dark star Petit Verdot with them is inspired and unexpected. But it works. Like most good north Italian reds, after a bitter, withdrawn start, black chocolate scrunched together with raw damson skins, the wine reluctantly begins to sweeten in the mouth, slowly revealing a ripe rosa plum fruit, cocoa powder sprinkled on the flesh, and then the tug of the French Petit Verdot finally releases a haunting, fragile scent of mint and violets.

16 2006 Sauvignon Blanc, Floresta, Santa Rita, Leyda Valley, Chile, 14% ABV

♦ Berkmann, Waitrose, £9.99

New Zealand may still be the leader in the world Sauvignon Blanc stakes, but Chile is making a determined run on the rails. You need cool conditions to produce good Sauvignon Blanc, and Chile is planting more and more coastal land where the air is chilled right down by the icy Humboldt Current that flows up South America's coast from the Antarctic. These foggy, windy areas are redefining the thrilling, crunchy greenness that makes Sauvignon such a refreshing drink. The Leyda Valley is about as close as you can get to the coast and this wine tingles on your tongue. It smells of tomato leaf, blackcurrant leaf and gooseberries and the flavour is a torrent of lime, green apple, nettle and gooseberry all washing over a pebbly riverbed. Big, powerful, sharp, green and spanking fresh.

17 2004 Shiraz, Turkey Flat, Barossa Valley, South Australia, 15% ABV
  ♦ Oz Wines, £19.99

This is the kind of Shiraz that I would frequently describe as just too much of a good thing. But then I see on the label that these vines were planted in 1847. Surely that makes them the oldest Shiraz vines in the world. Might they be the oldest wine vines of any sort in the world? Age must be revered and respected. Age may make whatever style of wine it will. And this is a rich, dense, earthy stew of a hundred and sixty summers, smelling as rustic yet exciting as a fancied stallion sweating before a race, tasting of damsons and plums mixed with red cherries and black chocolate, seasoned with pepper and thyme and a fistful of ancient soil crumbled into the cauldron and simmered until nightfall under the blazing Australian sky.

18 2005 Moulin-à-Vent, Château de Chénas, Beaujolais, France, 13% ABV
  ♦ Waitrose, £9.99

When will we forgive poor Beaujolais for the indignities heaped upon it in the name of Beaujolais Nouveau on all those dark November mornings over the years? The trouble is, all the beauty and excitement of Beaujolais' best wines got lost in the flood of mediocrity. But the flavour of Beaujolais' best is such a modern flavour, a perfect flavour for many of us who are beginning to tire of the full-frontal attack of vanilla oak, high alcohol and, frequently, some sugar left in the wine. Good Beaujolais is exuberant, it gurgles down your throat, the flavours laugh and skip with a rustic joy that makes you think the very soil is perfumed. This example is from Beaujolais' most serious village. Serious! Seriously delicious. Seriously irresistible, a great gushing tide of raspberries and loganberries, pear and banana all tumbling over the mineral dust of Beaulolais' dreamtime hills. If you're looking for an excuse to come back to Beaujolais, this is it.

19   2005 Soave, La Rocca, Pieropan, Veneto, Italy, 13% ABV
♦ Liberty Wines, £19.95

Is this really Soave? If you thought Soave was a drab, lifeless, thin white wine sold in large bottles for not very much money at your corner store, well, much Soave is. Just as much red Bordeaux is thin, muddy dreck, just as much Californian Merlot tastes as though it's been passed through a charcoal filter to make sure it doesn't taste of anything. And then there's Pieropan, just as there's Château Margaux in Bordeaux and Newton Californian Merlot. You could say Pieropan transcends everything Soave stands for. I'd prefer to say he shows how good Soave could be if more producers were prepared to use only the best vineyards and make their wine with care and dedication. With Pieropan, it's the texture that always strikes me, and the way that the flavour lingers timelessly in your mouth. This flavour starts with soft apple flesh, which dries out to stones then broadens and fattens like fluffed-up rice to a brilliant fruit finish that somehow marries custard apples with strawberry.

20   2005 Pinot Noir, Hatter's Hill, Delta Vineyard, Marlborough, New Zealand, 14.5% ABV
♦ Liberty Wines, £13.99

New Zealand is making some inspiring Pinot Noir. Disregarded as a serious red producer as little as a decade ago, the South Island has an ever-increasing band of superb Pinot Noirs, no longer trying to ape Burgundy, but powerfully proclaiming their own personalities. Marlborough, the Sauvignon Blanc centre, also produces the largest number of Pinot Noirs, and Hatter's Hill is made by Neil Ibbotson – who also makes supremely good Sauvignon. This has an unctuous texture, the fruit is rich and turbo-charged red strawberries and loganberries at their ripest and most assertive, washed lightly with honey and sprinkled with pepper.

21 2003 Shiraz Reserve, Ross Estate, Barossa Valley, South Australia, 14.5% ABV

🔻 Laithwaites, £17.99

Classic Barossa style, pushing the boundaries of ripeness until you feel sure they've gone too far – and then drawing back from the raisiny, stodgy abyss of overripeness. But how could you want more ripeness than this? It's suffused with rich chocolate, sweet prune and black plum, coconut and double cream, and the longer you hold it in your mouth the more perfume and richness appear, the rose water from Fry's Turkish Delight, black cherry and lingering damson. And then you notice there is some tannic bitterness. But by then you don't much care.

22 2005 Grüner Veltliner, Smaragd Kollmitz, Machherndl, Wachau, Austria, 13.5% ABV

🔻 Great Western Wine, £10.95

Fantastically refreshing white from the great Grüner Veltliner grape grown on the steep hills of the Wachau looking down to the Danube. This is bright, sunny, yet cool. Clean and yet full. with a real sense of the place – bleached stones and rocky crags. There is a lovely pale fruit too – fluffy ripe apple flesh – but the real excitement lies in the amazing savoury crunch of celery, white pepper and white radish.

23 2005 Shiraz-Grenache-Mourvèdre, Plexus, John Duval Wines, Barossa Valley, South Australia, 14.5% ABV

🔻 Liberty Wines, £16.95

John Duval used to make the legendary Grange red for Penfolds in the good old days. Now he's gone independent, which is Penfolds' loss and his gain, because in his new-found liberty he's gone back to the three great old Barossa Valley red varieties – Grenache, Syrah and Mourvèdre – and crafted a phenomenally lush red with a texture as dense as syrup. The flavours are all rich and black – black plums and prunes, black chocolate, liquorice and Fowler's Black Treacle roughed up with the rasp of fresh herbs.

24 2005 Chardonnay, Stoneleigh, Marlborough, New Zealand, 14.5% ABV
⬥ Threshers, £8.49 (3 for 2, £5.66)

This is a great Chardonnay bargain when you buy it as 3 for 2. New Zealand makes some of the world's best Chardonnays, often in quite small volumes, but this is made in decent quantities, to a very high standard, by a division of the global giant Pernod Ricard. It combines intense fruit with really 'Burgundian' oak flavours. What does this mean? OK: the fruit is bright and fresh, melons and eating apples, juicy but pale. The oak aging has added an almost syrupy richness of oatmeal, brazil nuts, toasted cashews and a texture of beeswax. And that's special.

25 2005 Bush Vine Grenache, Yalumba, Barossa, South Australia, 14.5% ABV
⬥ Berkmann, £8.99, Oz Wines and other independent retailers, £9.50

Grenache is a grape designed to make your head spin. It soaks up the sun and works at a frantic rate to convert the rays into sugar. The grapes bulge on the vine, squeal with delight as they're crushed and hurled into the fermenter, where they fight with each other to produce the most alcohol, the juiciest taste. It sounds far-fetched, but 14.5% alcohol is quite restrained for Barossa Grenache, and I think it's about right, because this is an irresistible mishmash of strawberry sauce, baked loganberry jam tarts, mint and herb and hot stones splashed with chocolate. It makes my head spin just writing about it.

26 2005 Vie, on y est, Domaine Gramenon, Rhône Valley, France, 14.5% ABV
  ◆ les Caves de Pyrene, £13.65

Remarkable wine from a superb grower in the Côtes du Rhône (see Sierra du Sud, page 23). You're not really supposed to make a pure Viognier in the Côtes du Rhône appellation, but Gramenon has a parcel of lush Viognier that they certainly aren't going to rip out, so they release the wines as 'mere' Vin de Table – table wine, the lowest title you can give a French wine. And they charge you £13.65 for it! Well, it's worth it. This is sumptuously exotic stuff; it boasts a rich, almost oily, apricot sultriness, superripe, slightly bruised, and a yeastiness that starts to taste like brioche soaked in crème fraîche as the wine warms up. There's a wild-eyed, gypsy beauty about this wine, untamed, untameable.

27 2005 Syrah, TMV, Swartland, South Africa, 14.5% ABV
  ◆ Waitrose, £15.00

I wish we saw more reds like this coming out of South Africa. It shows the animal power combined with sensual beauty that I've often tasted from the barrel when I've been in the Cape, but which rarely seems to come north. Maybe it's the price: 15 quid is a lot of money, but Syrah from the mountainsides north of Cape Town is bursting with personality and this is Syrah firing on all cylinders – wonderfully rich, scented with violets, soaked in blackberries but also throbbing with a raw rocky power and a savoury stream of fish oil on new leather to create a surprising but very satisfying mouthful.

28 2005 Malbec-Corvina, Passo Doble, Masi Tupungato, Argentina, 13.5% ABV

◆ Oddbins, Tesco, £8.99

Fascinating stuff. Masi are one of the top producers of Valpolicella in Italy and they specialize in a wild but delicious red wine style in which a Valpolicella is refermented on the yeast lees of another, richer style of wine made partly from grapes dried on racks. Masi have set up a vineyard and winery in Argentina and, as well as the native Malbec, they have planted the Corvina from Valpolicella and then made the wine using this Italian method of refermenting it on the yeast lees. Its brilliance lies in the unlikely but extremely successful marriage of sweet and sour, bitter and soft. The heart of this wine is succulent damson and cherry cream, but your tongue is prickled by a fruit sourness and a lash of black bitterness that is surprisingly delicious and invigorating. If you age this for a year or two it will gain an impressive dark plum and prune syrup richness.

29 2006 Valpolicella Classico, Allegrini, Veneto, Italy, 13% ABV

◆ Liberty Wines, £7.99

Right, here's your chance to try the classic but modern style of Valpolicella. Allegrini make utterly delicious wines at various levels. This is their basic Valpolicella and it is one of Italy's most gluggable reds. It's so juicy – juicy cherry and red plum, it's scented with rosehip and as squashy and soft as a ripe banana – and yet through all this runs a vivid streak of fruit acid like the slightly sour skin of an underripe plum. And therein lies the magic.

30 2005 Carignan, Vin de Pays des Côtes Catalanes, Empreinte du Temps, Domaine Ferrer Ribière, Languedoc-Roussillon, France, 14% ABV
♦ Yapp Brothers, £9.15

Every time I see a label proclaiming that the wine is made from genuinely old vines I feel a little shiver of excitement – and relief. Because it means that one more priceless parcel of vines has been saved from the plough. Once they're ripped out – well, you've got a hundred years to wait before the new vines become really old. It's not rocket science. These vines are 130 years old this year. People aren't replanting Carignan, and it's only when the vines get really old that you can see their special character. But don't expect an easy ride from old Carignan. This is tannic, powerful, visceral stuff. There is a richness like peanuts coated in chocolate, there's the Mediterranean odour of bay leaves – and there's fruit – dark, dark red flavours, striving for the ripe richness of black fruits, but not achieving it – superripe cranberries, superripe redcurrants, red plums, not black – and above all the dense, rich, ancient power of vines that suck their strength from deep in the rocky soils of these parched hills.

31 2000 Shiraz, Stonewell, Peter Lehmann, Barossa, South Australia, 14.5% ABV
♦ Waitrose, £30

Peter Lehmann makes excellent wines at every price level (his Wildcard Shiraz is one of our recommended wines for less than a fiver – see page 93). But this is where he pulls out all the stops. Stonewell itself is a superb vineyard and Lehmann also buys in grapes from wizened old growers in the scrawny, drought-stressed vineyards of the western Barossa. But scrawny ancient vines produce small amounts of intensely flavoured fruit, and that's what Lehmann is after. And he gets it. This is rich, exciting, almost baked in its intensity, but there's wonderful fruit there too – blackberry, loganberry and a sweet-sour flavour that reminded me of Finnish cloudberry liqueur. This is soaked in black treacle and brushed with herbs, and tastes of the very heartbeat of the Barossa. And like that heartbeat, it only beats stronger and more fervently as you age it.

32 2004 Terrano, Carso, Zidarich, Friuli-Venezia Giulia, Italy, 11.5% ABV

♦ les Caves de Pyrene, £17.55

Wild stuff. This comes from a narrow sliver of land connecting Trieste with the rest of Europe. This is bandit country; always has been. The locals know that there is politically a boundary with Slovenia just a mile or two away, but the winemakers have never taken the frontier too seriously – there are many good grapes growing on the Slovenian side. Anyway, everyone has a Slavic name around here – Zidarich? How Italian is that? – and Terrano is a strain of the Slavic Refosco grape. Quite a few of the Refoscos I know are reasonably high in alcohol, but this is only 11.5% and this allows unbeatable flavours to emerge that would be spoilt by higher alcohol. The wine has a noble, haughty acidity and gaunt graphite and slate minerality over which is laid an unwilling, sober trail of lean blackberry, lean loganberry, chewy celery stalk and a Fighting Téméraire's worth of black peppercorn.

33 2004 Chardonnay Tamar Ridge, Tasmania, Australia, 13.5% ABV

♦ deFINE, Lay & Wheeler and other independent retailers, £11.95

Just when you thought it was safe to give up on Aussie Chardonnay, up comes this delightfully classy little number from Tasmania to remind you that Aussie Chardie at its best is world-beating stuff. This has an appetizing, cool texture – good lean acidity, taut as a piano wire, zingy and bright. The fruit is the cool white apples of a Tasmanian orchard mixed with a little lush honeydew melon, and the oak is evident, but I like it – roasted cashew nuts and fresh Sunday breakfast toast. Mature, delicious, likely to give Aussie Chardie a good name again.

34   2005 Chardonnay, Rustenberg, Stellenbosch, South Africa, 13.9% ABV
♦ Waitrose, £9.99

These guys make very good whites, both oaked and unoaked. They have fabulous vineyards climbing up the daunting mountain slopes behind a beautiful homestead, and they're ambitious.

It shows in the wine. All the richness of barrel fermentation and yeast lees stirring is here, but it doesn't overpower the fruit. You end up with a rich, nutty style with the fatness of baked cream coming from the oak and the lees. Oaky styles are less popular than they used to be, but this is how it should be done.

35   2006 Sauvignon Blanc, Philip Shaw no. 19, Orange, New South Wales, Australia, 13% ABV
♦ Waitrose, £11.99

What a fascinating take on Sauvignon from one of Australia's iconic winemakers, the man who created the great Rosemount Estate wines when they were the real thing,

but has now gratefully cut loose and started his own venture in the cool hills of Orange. It gets very cold up here – vineyards go as high as 1050 metres and they can get snow and sleet summer or winter. Which suits Philip Shaw perfectly for his Sauvignon. And the coolness really glistens in a fascinating array of herb flavours dominated by parsley and sage, fruit of the lemon zest and green apple family and a full-bodied texture that has the additional intrigue of just a hint of salt.

36 2005 Chassagne-Montrachet, 1er cru Morgeot, Domaine Lamy-Pillot, Burgundy, France, 13% ABV

♦ Waitrose, £28.00

Lamy-Pillot own only a tiny patch of land here, less than an acre, but it's bang in the middle of one of Chassagne's best plots, the first-growth Morgeot. And they've carefully crafted a beautiful gentle balanced Chassagne, not too oaky – only 30% of the barrels are new, and that's just enough to create a soft, deep, balanced style, strikingly blending hazelnut with the richness of cream and a twist or two of spice.

37 2004 Riesling, Julius, Henschke, Eden Valley, South Australia, 12.5% ABV

♦ Lay & Wheeler, £14.00

Henschke are famous for making some of Australia's greatest reds from some of her oldest vines – there's a patch of Shiraz called The Grandfather that dates back to the 1860s. But they've always made superb traditional Riesling too, proudly austere when young, but capable of aging magnificently for decades. This 2004 is still very young, aggressive almost, you can almost feel the cold stones rubbing together in the chilly earth. That, plus very assertive lemon zest and lemon juice and some green apple flesh, makes for a haughty but delicious Riesling.

38 2004 Shiraz, Sanguine Estate, Heathcote, Victoria, Australia, 14.5% ABV

♦ Great Western Wine, £16.95

Heathcote is a prime example of how a lot of Australia's best vineyard sites probably haven't been discovered yet. Of course, with Australia's rather belated realization that it is the driest continent on earth and they're running out of water, we may not see too many more potentially green sites being developed, but at least Heathcote was discovered in time. It has some of the oldest soil in Australia – 500 million years old – and surely the reddest. The sheep up there are all stained red, it's that bad. But it's great wine dirt, especially Shiraz dirt. Heathcote gives reds of profound depth but lush texture, and this is a riotous mix of eucalyptus, plump blackberries and blackcurrants and honeybread bathed in chocolate.

39 2006 Riesling, Watervale, Mount Horrocks, Clare Valley, South Australia, 13% ABV
   ◆ Liberty, £12.95

Many Clare Rieslings are of fine quality but just a little austere. Owner/winemaker Stephanie Toole applies the feminine touch at Mount Horrocks and keeps the zingy tang of grapefruit and lemon – a citrus cavalcade – but wraps it round with much gentler flavours of nut and pastry, apricot and apple, and tops it off with peach blossom scent.

40 2003 Vacqueyras, Cuvée Azalais, Domaine le Sang des Cailloux, Rhône Valley, France, 14% ABV
   ◆ Christopher Piper Wines, £13.52

Powerhouse wine from a powerhouse estate in a powerhouse vintage. You can taste the blazing sun of the 2003 summer in this wine, the grapes half-shrivelling in the heat, the gnarled old vines just able to pump enough lifeblood through their vines from roots buried deep in the rocky soil. Burly, dense, superripe, strewn with herbs and, as the name of the estate implies, thick with blood sucked from the stones.

100 FOR A TENNER OR LESS

One of the most encouraging statistics to emerge this year was that among the independent wine retailers the average purchase price for a bottle of wine was £7.24. Given that the obsession of so many supermarket and high street retailers is to avoid breaking the £4.99 barrier, this is good news. I've always felt that once you break away from these artificial .99p price points, the value and the personality of the wines is immediately more rewarding. And that goes for the supermarkets too. So I've chosen a hundred wines for a tenner or less. Some of them are only 6 quid – in which case, bloody brilliant. Others are dead on the tenner. But this is the true heart of the wine world, where the producer can make enough profit to prosper and we can find memorable flavours – and change from a tenner.

- I've divided this section into whites followed by reds, kicking off with wines at the top end of this price bracket.

- Rosé wines have their own section on pages 102–107.

WHITE WINE

2006 Colombard-Sauvignon Blanc, La Biondina, Primo Estate, McLaren Vale, South Australia, 12% ABV
Philglas & Swiggot, £10.15

Colombard is largely disregarded in the wine world as something of a junk grape, fit only for distilling into brandy. That isn't fair. In southern France, especially Gascony, it makes sharp but really tasty dry whites. And in the hot corners of the earth it has a priceless ability to hold on to its acidity even as the boiling sun does its damnedest to bake the life out of it. Well, McLaren Vale in South Australia is hot. And yet Biondina has a delightful flavour and sense of lemon zest and crunchy green apple wrapped in a full, ripe, dry, but fairly neutral cloak. Drunk young, that's what you get – lean but tasty. Given a little bottle age the Sauvignon kicks in with more fruit and the wine gets deeper and more exciting.

2001 Semillon, Mount Pleasant Elizabeth, McWilliam's, Hunter Valley, New South Wales, Australia, 11% ABV
Morrisons, £9.99

This is not the kind of wine you expect to come across as you amble up the aisles of a supermarket which until recently largely prided itself on how many bottles it stocked at £2.99. This is a great old-fashioned Aussie classic from the Hunter Valley near Sydney. It's low in alcohol and has a brilliant, unique flavour of custard and nectarines, brioche and peach, orange peel and leather washed with beeswax that lingers in your mouth long after you've swallowed.

2005 Marsanne, Tahbilk, Victoria, Australia, 13.5% ABV
Threshers, £9.99 (3 for 2, £6.66)

Marsanne is a grape from the Rhône Valley in France and it's often accused of being flabby and soft and in need of blending with its neighbour Roussanne. But it shines in deepest Victoria at Tahbilk – rich, certainly, but blithely balanced, honeysuckle-scented and with the fatness of runny honey and nut flesh dried out a little by leathery dust and sharpened just a touch by ripe lemon acid.

2005 Bourgogne Chardonnay, Domaine du Pavillon, Burgundy, France, 13% ABV
Oddbins, £9.99

'Bourgogne' on the label can cover a multitude of sins and can simply be a dustbin for any old vats that didn't work out. But this one comes from a single vineyard on the outskirts of Meursault village, some of whose vines are in the Meursault appellation. So you get a very attractive 'almost Meursault' for less than half price. It lacks the lush texture of the grand Meursaults but it does have a true flavour of oatmeal, dry peach and nut flesh with a touch of waxy texture that would deepen no end with a few years' age.

2006 Pinot Gris, Tinja, Lowe Family Wine, Orange, New South Wales, Australia, 14% ABV
Vin du Van, Friarwood of Leith and other independents, £9.95

Waving, not drowning, in a sea of entirely forgettable but clearly very popular Pinot Grigio, this Pinot Gris – note the different name, which usually implies a tastier

version of Pinot Grigio – stands out for how good and interesting Pinot Gris can be. From the high-quality, cool area of Orange, inland from Sydney, this has ripe apple and Comice pear fruit, taut citrus acidity and a mellow custard cream softness. Delightful now, it'll get even better with age – say, another year or two.

2005 Sauvignon Blanc-Semillon, Sandalford, Margaret River, Western Australia, 12.5% ABV
Oz Wines, £9.99

Sauvignon-Semillon is the famous Bordeaux white blend of grapes, but you could just as well say it's the famous Margaret River blend because they do it equally effectively in the far west of Australia. This is bone dry but full textured, less aggressive than a New Zealand or South African Sauvignon, with an appetizing smell of coffee bean and blackcurrant leaf and a mellow nutty flavour tinged with leather to soften the zesty, citrus snap.

2005 Blanc de Morgex et de la Salle, Vini Estremi, Valle d'Aosta, Italy, 11.5% ABV
les Caves de Pyrene, £9.28

'The highest vineyards in Europe' proclaims the label, and if they really are at 1,300 metres, nestled into the slopes of Mont Blanc (on the Italian side), well, that would put them 200 metres above the highest that Switzerland can offer. You learn something every day. Trouble is, I forget something every day too. I won't forget this wine, though, with its scything, high mountain pass acidity that wrestles with waxy nut and apple fruit, mashed up to make a mild, inoffensive cake into which nature has hurled a ladleful of cider vinegar to curdle its bourgeois intent, and this acidity then spreads out into a delicious craggy rock dust minerality and the merest hint of a shy, barely scented high pasture bloom.

2006 Chardonnay, McLean's Farm, Barossa Valley, South Australia, 13% ABV
Oz Wines, £8.99

Bob McLean is a big, beefy fellow, generous and jovial, and I thought his Chardonnay would reflect this big, bluff style. But Bob is also a keen observer of the tides that sweep wine styles back and forth, and he knows that we like our Chardonnays a little more subtle nowadays. So, despite the fruit coming from Kalimna – a vineyard famous for providing brawny, succulent Shiraz grapes to one of Australia's greatest red wines, Penfolds' Grange – this is gentle, scented with peach blossom, flavoured with apple and melon flesh. I'd almost say it was feminine, but Bob knows where I live. He'd never let me get away with it.

2006 Grüner Veltliner, Obere Steigen, Huber, Traisental, Austria, 12.5% ABV
Oddbins, £8.99

Many Grüner Veltliners are marked out by a strong and appetizing flavour of white pepper. This one is a little riper and softer than usual, and has a different way of expressing its freshess – a spritzy prickle on the palate, a scent of sandalwood that is bone dry, and full white flesh that has a little grapefruit pith sharpness but is mostly juicy and fat.

2006 Hatzidakis, Santorini, Greece, 13.5% ABV
Halifax Wine Company, Waitrose, £8.99

Santorini is one of the Mediterranean's great experiences: the remains of a vast volcanic eruption has left a heart-stopping crescent bay, mighty cliffs and dark grey volcanic ash now turned to soil. Such extreme surroundings should produce exceptional wines – and they do. Assyrtiko is the local grape, and its wines always have an unnerving rock dust rasp to them, a real mineral growl, but this is evened out by excellent ripe green apple and ripe lemon flavours, and a savoury scent halfway between pepper and lovage.

2006 Riesling, Polish Hill River, O'Leary Walker, Clare Valley, South Australia, 12.5% ABV
Waitrose, £8.99

My mum's name is O'Leary, so I was always going to like this one. It shows the fascinating paradox of Clare Valley Riesling – able to be aggressive and snappy yet reassuringly full (*not* a description of my mum). Strong, stony green apple fruit is given extra gooseberry and lemon zest snap and then fattened up with the flesh of a baked apricot.

2004 Riesling, Show Reserve, Arrowfield Estate, Great Southern, Western Australia, 12.5% ABV Oddbins, £8.99

A Riesling from the broad empty acres of Western Australia's bottom end. The potential for quality is tremendous down here: the trouble is there is hardly any water available – and, of course, with no people, no passing trade to help the cashflow. Even so, what wine they do manage to squeeze out of their cool but arid earth is delicious. This is lovely Riesling – quite rich in texture, but this glycerine softness is easily overwhelmed by a citrus slap of lime zest, the rasp of vineyard stones and the passing whiff of petrol spilt from the pump.

2003 Les 4 Cépages (Gros Manseng, Chardonnay, Sauvignon, Semillon), Vin de Pays des Côtes de Gascogne, Tariquet, Famille Grassa, South-West France, 12% ABV
Threshers, £8.99 (3 for 2, £5.99)

Four wildly differing grape varieties put to original use in France's far South-West to come up with a really tasty blend that is full and rich but dry. It's as though we start with a toasty, nutty Chardonnay, but then extra layers are piled on: smoky apple, apricot, smoke drifting across peaches, leather, and the dry, chalky Gascony earth.

2006 Corse Sartène, Domaine Saparale, Corsica, France, 13% ABV
Yapp Brothers, £8.95

A full, proud, breast-beating white from the extremely self-willed island of Corsica. The Vermentino grape is best known for making dry, slightly snappy but fairly neutral whites. Here we see this relatively neutral variety at full extension. Green apple flesh, boiled lemons, grapefruit tartness, even a little tannic bitterness, softened yet never dumbed down by the slippery savouriness of yeast.

2006 Sauvignon Blanc-Semillon, Harewood Estate, Denmark, Western Australia, 12% ABV
Great Western Wine, Noel Young and other independent retailers, £8.95

This is the kind of wine I'd like to serve to all those vineyard owners and winemakers who seem determined to push ripeness – and therefore alcohol levels – far beyond what any sensible wine drinker desires. This is 12% alcohol – and all the better for it. It has attractively high lemon acidity but loads of cooked gooseberry fruit and coffee bean scent ruffled with a breeze of rock dust. It's full. It's green, and it's deliciously refreshing. It wouldn't be at 13.5%.

2006 Viognier-Pinot Gris, Heartland, Langhorne Creek-Limestone Coast, South Australia, 13.5% ABV
deFINE, Great Western Wine, Oddbins, Playford Ros, Selfridges, Tanners, Noel Young and other independent retailers, £8.95

All the lushness of Australian fruit with none of the sullen oak. This is delectable and inspiringly original in flavour – scented pear and apricot flesh, pithy lemon acidity and uplifting lime flower aroma to titillate your nostrils.

2006 Chablis, Domaine Servin, Burgundy, France, 12.5% ABV
Majestic, £8.49

Ah, what a delight. The calm, cool voice of reason – a lightly chilled, bone dry, well-mannered wine. It's soft, but only in terms of not sporting rough edges or rawness, it has lovely fluffy apple fruit, the acidity of ripe lemon peel and a cool undertow of pebbles. Mmm.

2006 Mâcon-Uchizy, Raphaël Sallet/Domaine de l'Arfentière, Burgundy, France, 13% ABV
Roger Harris Wines, £8.45

Uchizy is one of the best villages in the Mâconnais, but one of the least known – probably because it sounds like an invalid sneezing. Consequently you can get real Burgundy class for a fair price. This is delightful wine, not overblown, keenly balanced, a mix of ripe apple and slightly unripe peach before it's really softened, a soothing texture of savoury cream and a splash of honey.

2006 Chardonnay, Twin Wells, Hunter Valley, New South Wales, Australia, 13% ABV
Marks & Spencer, £7.99

Hunter Valley Chardonnays from north of Sydney were the first Aussie Chardonnays to become famous in Britain, but that was a long time ago and we'd find them pretty yellow and oily nowadays. Modern Hunter Chardonnays are still on the fat side, but far better balanced. This is a good example, with a leather and beeswax texture, gentle apple and nut fruit flavour and a warm-climate aroma of smoke tinged with a wisp of petrol fumes.

2005 Chardonnay, Hacienda el Espino 1707, Almansa, Castilla-La Mancha, Spain, 14% ABV
The Real Wine Company, £7.99

I know that Chardonnay can make a reasonable fist of things in most conditions, arctic to arid, but I didn't expect this to be one of them – Almansa is inland from the boilerhouse conditions of Alicante and Valencia in southern Spain. But then I discovered that this Chardonnay was grown on a limestone outcrop 750 metres high and hardly given any oak aging, and it made more sense – loads of sun, high-altitude coolness and Chardonnay's favourite soil type. The result is a very attractive, rather original wine – mild and full with an unlikely combination of baked apple flesh squashiness compounded by that indulgent dribbly scented flavour of a Williams pear at its peak.

2006 Riesling, Tim Adams, Clare Valley, South Australia, 12% ABV
Tesco, £7.99

If you want to experience the pure, crystalline nature of Australian Riesling, Tim Adams does it as well as any. His wine is full, but dry and austere, minerally dry flecked with lemon sherbet, green apple core and lime zest. Chill it down. Love it.

2005 Riesling, Magnus, Leasingham Wines, Clare Valley, South Australia, 12.5% ABV
Sainsbury's, Somerfield, Threshers, Noel Young, £7.99

Leasingham is a big operation and they make big-boned Rieslings, which is a bit paradoxical: weight, power and citrus delicacy. You find quite a lot of paradoxes – between light and weighty, green-scented and jam-rich – in Australia's Clare Valley, in both reds and whites. This still has loads of lemon and orange peel zip, apple and melon fruit, but also a little leathery fatness and petrol tank aroma.

2006 Sauvignon Blanc, M'Hudi, Elgin, South Africa, 13% ABV
Marks & Spencer, £7.99

I met the guys who make this wine last year. It's a Black Empowerment project. Sometimes you think the political purpose outweighs the wine quality, but sometimes you just know this one will work. M'hudi's like that. The guys are top guys, using top grapes from the cool highlands of Elgin. And the wine has that smashing, fizzing, ultra-green quality of good Cape Sauvignon. It's very dry, but attractively soft, yet the flavour is a rip-tide of nettles and coffee beans, lime leaf and juicy green apple.

2006 Sauvignon Blanc, Limited Selection, Montes, Leyda Valley, Chile, 13.5% ABV
Majestic, £7.99

Montes makes several Sauvignons, but this is my favourite – from the foggy coastal vineyards of Leyda, an area which is proving to be a star performer, particularly for Sauvignon and Pinot Noir. This is all green and fresh and outdoors. Nectarine and greengage, green apple, lime zest and nettles all crunch together with a mineral coolness.

2006 Viognier, Brampton (Rustenberg), Coastal Region, South Africa, 15.5% ABV
Tanners, £8.99, Waitrose, £7.99

Viognier isn't easy to grow, and it's surprisingly difficult to extract the exotic scents and lush fruit from young vine fruit without extracting tannic bitterness as well. But this wine is made by Rustenberg, white wine aces in Stellenbosch. Despite young vines, this is purring with fat, juicy apricot fruit and sour cream softness. There's quite a bit of alcohol and oak too, but the gobstopper fruit sails through.

2005 Pinot Gris, Irvine, Barossa Valley, South Australia, 14.5% ABV
Playford Ros, £7.95

I didn't know Pinot Gris grew in the Barossa Valley. Then I checked the small print and saw the grapes came from the much cooler Eden Valley in the hills to the east of Barossa. *That* makes sense. Eden Valley produces a range of wonderful white grapes. Why not Pinot Gris? This is the real thing – golden, low in acidity, with a mellow squashy apple and goldengage fruit, a hint of leather and mint, a wisp of smoke, a dab of honey and still dry. Very louche, I'd say.

2006 Albariño, Rías Baíxas, Val do Sosego (Bodegas As Laxas), Galicia, Spain, 12.5% ABV
Oddbins, £7.49

White from Spain's cool, wet north-west, where the Atlantic storms dump more rain than in Manchester. Thankfully it's also hotter than Manchester, so grapes can ripen, up to a point. But they never lose the sense of cool and moisture. This wine is soft, even slightly chubby, but that only serves as a vehicle for the cool fruit of pears and white peach and the pithy bitterness of grapefruit zest. And all the time you sense the grass glistening with dew, the cliff rocks washed with rain.

2005 Chardonnay, Fairleigh Estate, Marlborough, New Zealand, 14.5% ABV
Majestic, £7.49

If you want an oaky Chardonnay, New Zealand provides much more fruit and acidity to go with the oak than most countries. This has lovely pear and peach fruit, soft, nutty, spicy oak and a lively acidity. Slightly old style, but very good.

2006 Sauvignon Blanc, Classic Reserve, Viña Leyda, Leyda Valley, Chile, 13.5% ABV
Playford Ros, £7.49

This is marvellous tangy stuff, a great riot of green sharp flavours, yet the end sensation is ripe, not raw. Grapefruit and gooseberry, passionfruit and blackcurrant leaf, lime zest and nettles all foaming over your tongue like a wave breaking along the beach.

2005 Gros Manseng-Sauvignon, Vin de Pays des Côtes de Gascogne, Alain Brumont, South-West France, 12.5% ABV Green & Blue, £7.45

Alain Brumont is a great red wine producer in France's South-West, but he's decided on a very interesting white combination here – the sharp Gros Manseng and the aromatic Sauvignon – and it works. It's a lovely, full, challenging mix of tropical and green, nectarine and peach and pear in an off-dry relationship with lemon zest and leaves plucked from a pepper tree.

2005 Mtsvane, Tamada, Georgia, 12.5% ABV
Laithwaites, £7.39

Like the Georgian red on page 65, this is modern wine with an inheritance stretching back to the beginning of wine time. But in those days the wine would have been brown, probably fermented and stored in hollowed-out tree trunks. Worth trying once. More than that and life-long abstinence becomes a real possibility. This one is good, though, with a fascinating flavour of rich spiced Bramley apple purée, stewed marrow and the world-weary autumn richness of medlars and quince.

2005 Chardonnay, Vin de Pays d'Oc, Advocate, Domaine Saint Hilaire, Languedoc-Roussillon, France, 13.5% ABV
Christopher Piper Wines, £7.26

Spot-on Chardonnay for those of you who don't like the thick-headed stodgy style so many New World Chardonnays have adopted. This wine is from an excellent single estate in southern France. It does have some oak influence, but very subtly applied, in the French manner: melon and apple fruit – fresh, not squashy – a little apple peel rasp to sharpen the palate, and a mild, spicy, nutty oak veneer that makes no attempt to dominate the wine.

2006 Riesling, Danny Schuster, Waipara, New Zealand, 10.5% ABV
les Caves de Pyrene, £7.04

Given that Australia makes many superb Rieslings in relatively warm conditions, the cool-loving Riesling really should be seen more in New Zealand. Maybe its relative scarcity is simply because we won't buy it. Well, Waipara is well down the South Island towards Christchurch – brilliant cool conditions – and this delicate, fragrant example is a delight: only 10.5% alcohol and an absurdly drinkable mélange of orange, lime and peach, scratched with the mineral lick of stones and not quite dry.

2005 Chardonnay, Yering Frog, Yering Station, Yarra Valley, Victoria, Australia, 14% ABV
Majestic, £6.99

Balance is what marks the delicate but tasty Chardonnays of the Yarra Valley near Melbourne. Gentle, spicy oak marries effortlessly with a soft, almost dilute, acidity, mellow apple fruit and a warm cream and nut syrup softness. Everything in balance. The Yarra Valley is a very expensive area, yet this is a quid or two less than the rubbish South East Australian Chardonnays that bestrew the high street. Of course, this holds its price. No one in their right mind buys the rubbish brands until they're slashed to £3.99.

2006 Sauvignon Blanc, Secano Estate, Leyda Valley, Chile
Marks & Spencer, £6.99

I'm delighted to see the wines of Leyda spreading rapidly into the high street and the supermarkets. This brand new coastal area of Chile hit the ground running with some of the most spanking fresh Sauvignons the world had seen only a couple of years ago. As the vines have got older, the wines have become fuller, but lost none of their brilliantly, aromatically aggressive turmoil of capsicum, gooseberry, celery, nettle and lime zest. Exhilarating stuff.

2006 Sauvignon Blanc, Ormonde Cellars, Darling, South Africa, 12% ABV
Tesco, £6.99

All up the west coast of South Africa we're discovering more and more excellent cool-climate sites that particularly shine with Sauvignon. The flavours are different to those of New Zealand: they're leaner, more aggressive, less full of tropical fruit and lime zest. This is a good example, from the Darling Hills – tangy but full-bodied, with the sharpness of nettles, the juiciness of green apples and the drying flavours of summer earth and freshly roasted coffee beans.

2006 Sauvignon Blanc, Dashwood, Marlborough, New Zealand, 13.5% ABV
Oddbins, £6.99

One of the most consistently high quality yet affordable Kiwi Sauvignons on the market. I use it in tastings all around the country and it never lets me down. It pings with mouthwatering green-fleshed fruit – apples and lime, nettles and gooseberry and even an exotic drop of passionfruit. Ripe and tangy. Very good.

2006 Sauvignon Blanc, Explorers Vineyard, New Zealand, 13% ABV
Co-op, £6.99

The Explorers label is always worth seeking out at the Co-op; like the Dashwood (above), this is one of the best-priced Kiwi Sauvignons in the country. It's got good stabbing gooseberry, lime zest and nettles and a streak of metallic mineral. Full bodied, but aggressively zesty with it.

2006 Chardonnay Reserva, Viña Porta, Bío Bío Valley, Chile, 13.5% ABV
Threshers, £6.49 (3 for 2, £4.33)

An intelligent mix of Chardonnay grapes from Bío Bío in the cool damp south and Chile's much warmer Central Valley. There's no splodge of oak to detract from the flavours, so you get a very easy, pleasant, fresh style dominated by pear, apple and melon flesh tarted up with a flicker of spicy cream.

2006 Cheverny, Le Vieux Clos, Delaille, Loire Valley, France, 12.5% ABV
Majestic, £6.49

What a delightful surprise. This is 85% Sauvignon and 15% Chardonnay from what can only be described as one of the lesser byways of the Loire Valley. But it's delicious. It's aggressive, but that's exactly what most boring modern Loire whites lack. This is a riot of pith and leaf (pronounce that after a couple) – blackcurrant leaf, grapefruit and lemon pith, white melon flesh, coffee bean scent – all just softened a little by the 15% Chardonnay. I remember not too long ago when Sancerre used to make wines like this. Until she remembers how to, I shall have to drink Cheverny.

2006 Fiano-Greco, A Mano, Puglia, Italy, 12.5% ABV
Booths, Hedley Wright, Philglas & Swiggot, Villeneuve, Noel Young and other independent retailers, £6.49

Delightful coupling of two of southern Italy's most interesting grape varieties from the unlikely arid area of the heel of Italy – Puglia. You'd expect Puglian whites to be bleached and baked by the sun, but this one is spritzy fresh, with loads of fruit flavour, a touch of floral scent, a gentle acidity like boiled lemons – zest and all – backed up by pastry softness.

2006 Sauvignon Blanc, The Best, Curicó Valley, Chile, 13% ABV
Morrisons, £6.49

The label says this Sauvignon is from the warm Curicó Valley, but I'll wager good money there's more than a splash of high-quality cool-climate fruit in the blend, because the ripeness is matched with streaks and shards of grapefruit pith, green apple and lemon zest.

2006 Chardonnay, Block 66, Kingston Estate, Padthaway, South Australia, 13.5% ABV
Averys, £6.29

Here's a producer who understands quality, personality and a sensible price. I associate Kingston Estate with full-blooded reds, not Chardonnay. Never mind. Down in the fairly upmarket region of Padthaway, famous for very serious Chardonnays, they've come up with a very attractive spicy modern Chardie with just a hint of that traditional leather and fat fruit Aussie thing. It's fresh, it's bright and it has an aftertaste of peach blossom scent in spring.

2006 Albariño, Rías Baíxas, Galicia, Spain, 12.5% ABV
Sainsbury's Taste the Difference, £5.99

This is a little chubbier than I expected, but that isn't too much of a problem, because the traditional Galician austerity soon muscles past the puppy fat, the stewed, barely ripe apple fruit turns towards mint perfume and stones and the final effect is of the rocky coastline, the wild Atlantic weather and a flavour washed endlessly by fresh summer rain.

2005 Bergerac Sec, Sauvignon Blanc-Sémillon, Domaine des Eyssards, South-West France, 13% ABV Waitrose, £5.99

Bergerac's vineyards are basically the same as Bordeaux's; it's purely an administrative boundary between the *départements* of Gironde and Dordogne that demands a change of name. The grapes they grow are the same and this Sauvignon-Sémillon – the classic white Bordeaux blend – has good waxy weight from the Sémillon and a spring shower of sharp green flavours and scents: capsicum, nettle, blackcurrant leaf and grapefruit as well as the juicy fruit of ripe apple and pear. There's even a touch of spritz to tingle your tongue.

2005 Coteaux du Languedoc, Picpoul de Pinet, Domaine de Félines, Languedoc-Roussillon, France, 13% ABV Waitrose, £5.99

I never quite know how Picpoul de Pinet manages to make such fresh wine in such a torrid part of France's Mediterranean coast, but it's been famous for generations as the far south's smartest white. Well, the grape's name gives you a clue: Picpoul means 'lipstinger' in old French, and it's one of the few white grapes

that could keep its acidity in such super-hot conditions. Most Picpoul is made by the co-op and is fair, but single estates are much better. This has a very nice apple and pear flavour, maybe the apple is just a little bruised, and there's a pleasant hint of almond. And the acidity? It's there.

2005 Unoaked Chardonnay, Explorers Vineyard, New Zealand, 13% ABV Co-op, £5.99

Oak can be used to hide the deficiencies in Chardonnay fruit: the vanilla and spice of barrels provides great make-up. So if you're going to make a successful *un*oaked Chardonnay, the fruit must be of good quality. In which case New Zealand is a good place to go, since she grows some of the world's best Chardonnay. This one has delightful greengage and apple fruit, fattened up with some nuts, and honeyed from having its creamy yeast lees stirred up with the wine in the tank, and there's a slight suggestion of white pepper.

2006 Vin de Pays des Coteaux de Murviel, Cépage Rolle, Domaine de Coujan, Languedoc-Roussillon, France, 14% ABV
Great Western Wine, £5.95

Characterful white grapes are a bit hard to find around the Mediterranean coast – it's much more a red wine stronghold. But Rolle is an excellent southern French variety we should see more of. This is dry but full, almost waxy in texture, but with a fruit jellyish kind of flavour – pink apple jelly, lemon jelly – and the Mediterranean makes itself felt with a hint of tannin and rocks sprayed by the sea.

2006 Riesling, Budai, Nyakas, Hungary, 12.5% ABV
Wines of Westhorpe, £5.70

Hungary isn't known for its Riesling, but it does have many cool vineyard areas where Riesling might thrive. I could mistake this for an Australian Riesling – that's a compliment – because it's bone dry, with a concentrated green apple peel, greengage and grapefruit core, sharp lemon peel acidity and the rough rub of stones.

RED WINE

2004 Crozes Hermitage, Domaine Yann Chave, Rhône Valley, France, 13.5% ABV
Laithwaites, £10.15

Remarkable wine – a wild, medicinal rollercoaster, perhaps because some of the grapes weren't totally ripe, perhaps simply because M. Chave is a wacky kind of guy. When you open the bottle, the smell is like Fisherman's Friends and Vicks Vapour Rub, but there is crunchy red plum and stewed bilberry fruit and a talc and custard cream smoothness, Bizarre? It is. If it sounds too much for you, decant it for a few hours and a more classic Crozes of blackberry, cream and violet perfume will hint at emerging.

2004 Cabernet-Merlot 'The Cracker!', Hope Estate, Western Australia, 13% ABV
Threshers, £9.99 (3 for 2, £6.66)

This is made by the Hope Estate from the Hunter Valley near Sydney, where a fat, lush style is usual. They've imported some of that tendency to the more restrained acres of Western Australia, where they've crafted a rich, ripe red in the style of Bordeaux's Pomerol, with ladlesful of juicy blackcurrant jam and clotted cream indulgence and a welcome nip of acidity that merely serves to emphasize the delightful fruit.

2006 Pinot Noir, Stoneleigh, Marlborough, New Zealand, 13% ABV
Threshers, £9.99 (3 for 2, £6.66), Waitrose, £8.99

If Chile is a new star for Pinot Noir, so is New Zealand. This is made by the giant Pernod Ricard operation and it shows the big boys can do good if they want to. Luckily, at Stoneleigh in New Zealand's Marlborough region, they seem to want to. This is a serious Pinot Noir, rather like red Burgundy in style, but much cheaper. It's probably not at its best for a year or two, but it's already displaying lovely cherry and strawberry fruit, fair acidity and a gentle oak influence like brioche and the slightly burnt top of a rice pudding.

2006 Cabernet Sauvignon, Jester, Mitolo, McLaren Vale, South Australia, 14.5% ABV
Liberty Wines, £9.95

I worry sometimes when I read my tasting notes. What am I supposed to make of this: 'I'm tasting this and I feel as though there's a hurricane lancing in from my left.' I mean … what? It was late in the day. Some excuse. OK. This is pretty dense stuff – plum skins, dates and prunes – but it's saved from being OTT by a swish of herbs and a surprising streak of lemon zest.

2005 Crozes Hermitage, Papillon, Domaine Gilles Robin, Rhône Valley, France, 13% ABV
The Wine Society, £9.50

It's the sheer come-hither quality of good modern Crozes that is such a delight, especially when you think that close neighbour Hermitage is all about beef and brawn. They both use the Syrah grape, yet to completely different effect. This has the heady, ripe blackberry fruit and violet perfume of modern Crozes, fattened up with crème fraîche and, I thought, given a savoury twist a bit like Shippham's fish paste (yum – ed.).

2005 Brouilly, Château du Pavé, Beaujolais, France, 13% ABV
Christopher Piper Wines, £9.42

You've got to be keen on this when you read the label. The grapes come from a little three-hectare plot that has been in the same family since 1631. Since Beaujolais has been dirt poor for three and a half centuries of that time, that's pretty good going. So, what about the quality of the wine? Well, it's a charming, classy mix of mineral dryness and juicy red fruit – plum, raspberry, cherry – plucked off the tree just before ripeness, with a few squashy windfalls thrown in for good measure. With only three hectares, waste not want not.

2001 Barbera d'Asti Superiore, Trinchero, Piedmont, Italy, 13.5% ABV
Green & Blue, £9.00

The reds of Piedmont are some of Italy's most difficult to get to grips with, yet there *is* a certain magic about them – a hidden, sceptical beauty. You can't avoid acidity, or tannin, but if you mature the wine a few years, at least the fruit and oak will have developed some density and richness to combat their assault. This is still fairly tannic, it's still got a fair amount of acidity that somehow reminds me of lettuce (acid lettuce? No, I can't explain it). But there's a strange and wild stew of bletted autumn fruits, of red summer fruits now slightly staled by time and tossed with meat stock. And the stew would have been simmering for a long time in an open cauldron, and hardly stirred once.

2005 Bordeaux Supérieur, Château Pey La Tour Reserve, Bordeaux, France, 14.5% ABV
Waitrose, The Wine Society, £8.99

This is the reserve 'special treatment' wine of a very good property in the middle of nowhere, owned by the big Dourthe company. The land must be good because the wine reaches 14.5% alcohol – that's almost

obscene, even in a star year like 2005.
Certainly the flavour is sumptuous for what
is technically a lesser growth: cream mixing
with soft fat plums and shiny leather and
chocolate, the whole thing just about held in
check by a light pebble earthiness. Is this the face of Bordeaux in the
global warming future?

2005 Bordeaux, Lurton La Chapelle, Bordeaux, France, 13.5% ABV
Marks & Spencer, £8.99

The fabled 2005 vintage is showing its true
worth by sending a shoal of wines from
lesser vineyard sites that are marked by
ripeness and style – something that is
usually in short supply in Bordeaux outside
the famous properties. This is quite powerful stuff but it's soft and
mellow too, with a rich, gentle toffee and cream flavour dominating, just a
flicker of leafy acidity and a sprinkling of fine, dusty summer earth.

2005 Pillar Box Red, Henry's Drive, Padthaway, South Australia, 15% ABV
Threshers, £8.99 (3 for 2, £5.99)

Thick, dense, wonderful winter red that I had several times last year in the freezing cold – and it did me no
end of good. It's a stonking 15% alcohol – normally too much for me – but although it's bursting with
unctuous syrupy red plum fruit and creamy chocolate goo, it has a most surprising and refreshing streak of
acidity too. If it's balanced, I can take 15%.

2002 Rioja Reserva, Elegia (Torre de Oña/La Rioja Alta), Spain, 13.5% ABV
Sainsbury's Taste the Difference, £8.99

Over the years (rather a lot of them) Rioja Alta has been my favourite Rioja producer more often than any other, able to produce sublime top-end wine as well as big-volume blends that still display some of the class of the far more expensive bottlings. And for as long as I can remember, Sainsbury's have used them to supply their own-label Rioja. Long may it continue. This is the best type of traditional Rioja – the type we Brits love – not dark and tough and drenched with aggressive oak, but gentle, soothing, easy to appreciate, and swimming in squashy strawberry and peach flesh fruit, coated in savoury cream and coconut and very lightly dusted with earth.

2005 Vacqueyras, Domaine Bastides d'Eole, Rhône Valley, France, 14% ABV
Marks & Spencer, £8.99

Big, beefy red. This gets better and better if you open the bottle (and pour out a little) an hour before you drink it. Vacqueyras is one of the important villages near Châteauneuf-du-Pape in the southern Rhône. The wines are much cheaper, not quite so rich, but they're full of dark, powerful flavours, the fruit almost stewed by the heat, herbs of the hillsides – thyme and rosemary and bay – infuse the wine, and there's a bitter cleansing rasp halfway between black chocolate and sun-bleached stones.

2005 Montepulciano d'Abruzzo, Casale Vecchio, Abruzzo, Italy, 13% ABV
Laithwaites, £8.59

There's much cheaper Montepulciano d'Abruzzo around than this, but most of it is pretty rough stuff. Pay the extra and discover why the Italians rate the grape so highly. It's reasonably tannic, but the bitterness is swamped by a treacly tide of ripe black plums and toasty nut syrup, and that's matched by a remarkable cranberry and apple acidity and a refreshing dash of mineral dust.

2004 Minervois la Livinière, La Cantilène, Château Sainte-Eulalie, Languedoc-Roussillon, France, 14.5% ABV
The Wine Society, £8.50

La Livinière is the sweet heart, the perfumed core of the large Minervois region. At their best, these are some of the most lovely southern French reds, because of their perfume. This wine treads a tightrope between dense, chocolaty, black plum fruit and a wave of pepper and herbs, and rising above all this, the fragrance of violets and jasmine. That's some feat.

2004 Cabernet-Merlot, Knappstein, South Australia, 14.5% ABV
Oddbins, £8.49

A Cabernet Sauvignon-dominated red whose producer seems to have realized that Clare Valley Cabernet by itself might be a bit stern and so has used Merlot, but also the juicy Malbec and the raspberry-scented Cabernet Franc to create a much gentler, rounder glass of wine. It works. There's an attractive eucalyptus scent – often a sign of cool-climate Cabernet – and this is matched by a delightful blackcurrant and raspberry throat pastille jelly-soft fruit.

2005 Saperavi Reserve, Tamada, Georgia, 12.5% ABV
Laithwaites, £8.09

Now this is something for the courageous of heart. A wine from Georgia – and the Georgians say it was they who first made wine. Like, really first – 5000 years ago. I don't know what the Georgians' reputation for probity is, but old-style Georgian wine used to taste so bizarre it could well have been a first effort that no one had managed to improve upon. However, this is a modern version, and is seriously good. Saperavi is a fantastic grape that I tip for international stardom over the next 20 years. This wine is big and a little rough as yet; tannin and acid are quite evident, but they taste completely integrated and play a real part in the rich rush of red-fleshed plum and ripe cranberry fruit decked in black treacle and dreams of greatness.

2005 Carmenère, Atalaya, Edición Limitada, Viña La Rosa, Rapel, Chile, 14% ABV
Laithwaites, £7.99

I'm delighted at how many excellent Carmenères are coming onto the shelves, because this is a grape with a really different personality to the famous French grapes like Merlot and Cabernet Sauvignon. This one is rich, dark and savoury, ripe black fruit muddled together with celery and freshly ground pepper.

2005 Chiroubles, Georges Duboeuf, Beaujolais, France, 12.5% ABV
Averys, Waitrose, £7.99

Wow, the 2005 Beaujolais are tremendous, and luckily the 2006s aren't far off in quality. The trouble is, we don't seem to trust Beaujolais any more. Well, we really should try, and Duboeuf is a good place to start. He's the biggest – and one of the best – producer and his single village and single vineyard wines are

utterly delicious. Chiroubles is a village which usually makes quite delicate reds – but not in this instance: this is a deep, chewy, yet massively drinkable brew of stones and pebble dust, strawberries squashed in castor sugar, topped up with pear juice and cream.

2002 Conca de Barberà, Cabernet Sauvignon-Merlot, Marqués del Costal, Cataluña, Spain, 13.5% ABV
Marks & Spencer, £7.99

This is supposedly made from the French classic grape varieties Cabernet Sauvignon and Merlot. But you'd never know. The whole thing is bursting with Spanish ripeness – stewed plums and strawberries mixed with gooey caramel, cream just starting to curdle, and the rustic reassurance of warm summer earth.

2004 Oak Aged Durif, The Boxer, Bill Calabria (Westend Estate), New South Wales, Australia, 15% ABV
Laithwaites, £7.99

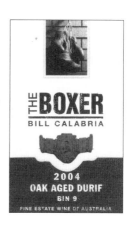

Durif doesn't flourish in many parts of the world, and in the few crannies that it does, the battle is to cool down its bitter aggression and peer inside to see if there's a fruity core. So I don't blame them for calling this The Boxer, but Durif is probably more at home in Australia's Riverina than anywhere else, and Calabria is a dab hand at prising open its sweet-fruited heart. This has a strong, stewy sweetness like the last squashy squeeze of ripe plum skins, it's nicely roughened by liquorice and fresh thyme and it has a tolerably evident acidity. You could age it too.

2004 Durif, Rutherglen Estates, Victoria, Australia, 14.5% ABV
Waitrose, £7.99

One of several Durifs that are appearing from the arid heat of Australia's inland vineyards, showing how well adapted it is to these extreme conditions. This is from the gold-rush area of Rutherglen, more famous for unbelievably sticky liqueur Muscats; but this Durif is red – or rather, almost black – muscular and unpretty at first glimpse but then a damson scent struggles through the bitter black chocolate carapace, and a blackcurrant and raisin depth slowly unfolds in the heart of the wine.

2005 Durif, El Gordo, Clare Valley, South Australia, 14.5% ABV
Oz Wines, £7.99

El Gordo means 'the fat one' – add big, dense, thick-set, rough-hewn to 'fat', and I'll drink to that. Durif is a beast in any case, rarely tamed, but these guys have just about managed it – the tannic chunkiness well matched by rich black plum syrup, herbs, eucalyptus and mint.

2006 Memsie (Shiraz-Cabernet Sauvignon-Malbec), Water Wheel, Bendigo, Victoria, Australia, 14.5% ABV
Oz Wines, £7.99

Memsie never sounds terribly serious. And it isn't. It's a gushing flood of all that's good about individually grown and produced Aussie reds. This has a gorgeous lush texture, blackberry and plums and morello cherries chastised with eucalyptus and then cosseted with baked caramel sauce on ice cream. Sheer pleasure.

2005 Petit Verdot-Syrah Reservado, Tarapacá, Maipo Valley, Chile, 14% ABV
Laithwaites, £7.99

This is a good idea. Petit Verdot is normally a fairly tannic grape whereas Syrah is usually fairly rich and soft in the New World. So blend them. If you're lucky, Petit Verdot will also contribute a haunting violet scent. Maybe next vintage: the perfume here is a rougher one of pepper and herbs, but the texture is full of deep ripe black fruit gingered up with savoury nut and then that pepper again.

2005 Pinotage, Houdamond, Bellevue Estate, Stellenbosch, South Africa, 14.5% ABV
Marks & Spencer, £7.99

Pinotage is a grape that arouses strong emotions, and I can see why, especially when one of its problems is a propensity to be teeth-chatteringly bitter. Not many makers succeed in taming it, but well done M&S, because this is a delight – a lovely dark red richness of raspberry sauce and mulberries, a smoky scent of marshmallows being toasted at a Guy Fawkes bonfire, and a biting depth of bitter chocolate.

2006 Pinotage, Diemersfontein, Wellington, South Africa, 14% ABV
Waitrose, £7.99

This wine really divides people. When it was first launched a few years ago its amazing chocolate and mocha coffee concentration of flavour seemed to herald a new dawn for Pinotage. Nowadays some people say they like mocha but, at this density, they'd rather go to Starbucks. I agree, it's a very coffee-chocolate-rich, dark wine and I would like to see the fruit a bit more evident, but it's still a helluva drink.

2004 Oak Aged Saint Macaire, Private Bin L19, Calabria (Westend Estate), Riverina, New South Wales, Australia, 14% ABV
Laithwaites, £7.99

Good old Calabria. Good old true blue Aussies. The Saint Macaire is an incredibly rare Bordeaux grape. They never thought much of it in Bordeaux, and I'd be amazed if it wasn't extinct there. But once a grape variety has been transplanted to the traditional areas of Australia, full of old-timers who hate uprooting a grape just because it isn't trendy, it'll survive until it dies of old age. Even so, this is the first time I've *ever* seen Saint Macaire on a wine label. The wine is big, rustic, with that Italian ability to mix dense, stewy, sweet yet acid black fruit with the smell of a horse sweating up and a handful of earth and mould scooped from the forest floor. Calabria's a good Italian name. He knows how.

2004 Shiraz, Toa, Coriole Vineyards, McLaren Vale, South Australia, 14% ABV
Flagship Wines, £7.99

Coriole are based in South Australia's McLaren Vale but they have never gorged themselves on the abundant overripe fruit available locally, unlike so many of their Adelaide area colleagues. This is certainly ripe and has good chunks of chocolate and toffee, dark cherry and smoky nut, but it never falls into the palate-fatiguing fault of overripeness. The label has a potato on it. Am I missing something? (yes, this is no potato but a fascinating piece of Aboriginal culture – read the back label – ed.)

2005 Shiraz Reserve, Buckingham Estate, Western Australia, 14.5% ABV
Morrisons, £7.99

The label's half in Latin and there's a damn great crown in the middle – what are they trying to suggest? That this is Prince Philip's home brew? Well, I'm sure he'd like it, because it's a good, dry Western Australian style, midweight, with ripe blackberry fruit and a flick of hillside herbs.

2005 Shiraz-Viognier, Zonte's Footstep, Langhorne Creek, South Australia, 14.5% ABV
Sainsbury's, Somerfield, £7.99

Talk about red wine without tears. This is gorgeous stuff. The fruit is scented and soft, raspberries and peaches, almost the kind of mild fruit you get in fruit gums, and it's softened even more by a confectioners' cream of the kind you find in chocolates. You may ask – is this a dry or sweet wine? It's dry, and there's a decent splash of smoky toast, leather and eucalyptus to ram the point home.

2005 Tempranillo, Barossa, Peter Lehmann, South Australia, 14.5% ABV
Waitrose, £7.99

Tempranillo has been one of the fastest-growing grape varieties in Australia for several years. I admit there was only about a shovelful to start with, but there are several hundred hectares now, and it's proving a real find. It's a Spanish grape, and I think the Spanish would be proud of this – rich strawberry and red cherry fruit, soft nutty weight, a rub of leather and a little tannic rasp. Pretty classic Tempranillo, I'd say.

2003 Costières de Nîmes, 'Les Cimels', Château d'Or et de Gueules, Rhône Valley, France, 14% ABV
The Real Wine Company, £7.55

Costières de Nîmes is the absolute southern end of the Rhône Valley and wasn't even thought of as part of it until a few years ago, when they revealed that they had soils blanketed with stones that were much like those of Châteauneuf-du-Pape. The wines aren't that similar, but Costières de Nîmes has rapidly carved a reputation for minerally, fruit-driven reds and delightful scented whites and rosés. This red is fairly dense, but full of rich red fruit like cranberries and red cherries stewed together, as well as a cleansing metallic pebbly quality and a brief swish of herbs.

2005 Australian Shiraz, The Best, Barossa Valley, South Australia, 14.5% ABV Morrisons, £7.55

Big, brawny stuff, not subtle, but am I bovvered? Subtle Barossa, I don't think so. Give me this big, dense soup of blackberry and plum jam, a rasp of herb, and toffee and chocolate just slightly burnt in the pan when they're being melted.

2005 Carmenère, Classic Reserve, Viña Leyda, Central Valley, Chile, 13.5% ABV Playford Ros, £7.49

Carmenère can knock you back on your heels and quietly wow you with its remarkable flavours. It'll never be subtle or elegant – it's not that sort of grape – but this is on the gentler side, pleasant white pepper, soy sauce and celery savouriness melding easily with blackcurrant fruit and caramel oak into a charming, restrained version – but still unmistakably Carmenère.

2006 Beaujolais, Cuvée Terroir, Domaine Chatelus, Beaujolais, France, 12% ABV
Roger Harris Wines, £7.35

Delightful proof that 2006 is another good Beaujolais vintage, with lovely gluggable juicy fruit to the fore. It's got that magical mix of strawberries, pears and stones that sounds unlikely but is *so* refreshing – pears dripping with juice, strawberries lifted from a summer pudding, pebbles bright and clean. Then I thought of pears in red wine with a drop or two of vanilla custard. Then I thought of talcum powder made from pebble dust. Then I thought I needed a cold shower.

2005 Cabernet Sauvignon, Equality by Las Lomas/Fairtrade, Maule Valley, Chile, 14% ABV
Threshers, £6.99 (3 for 2, £4.66)

Equality is a new Fairtrade label from Chile and the first wines are bursting with personality. This comes from a wild, sparsely populated southern valley and has more grip and attack than a typical Chilean Cabernet. But I don't mind that, because there's really strong direct blackcurrant fruit and exotic eucalyptus scent. Just show it to a big slab of char-grilled sirloin.

2004 Cabernet-Merlot Reserve, Palandri Estate, Western Australia, 14.5% ABV
Co-op, £6.99

A lovely example of why Western Australia is thought of as more European and restrained than the rest of Oz. It has that magic combination of ripe, fat, dewy blackcurrant and the lazily hot scent of eucalyptus, but it doesn't cloy, and the oak is merely a delicate brushstroke of toffee and nut on the surface of the dark perfumed fruit.

2005 Douro, Quinta do Crasto, Portugal, 14% ABV
Sainsbury's Taste the Difference, £6.99

Sainsbury's have gone to one of the best Douro producers for their Taste the Difference. Quinta do Crasto is perched on a heavenly spur above the majestic Douro river and makes ports and table wines to match its beautiful site. This is warm-blooded red, but it does exude a delicate fragrance of violets and, although the flavour is pretty ripe and hinting at raisins, the heart of the fruit is delicious soft juicy damsons.

2006 Syrah, Porcupine Ridge (Boekenhoutskloof), Cape of Good Hope, South Africa, 14.5% ABV
Waitrose, £6.99

A great example of how thrilling, yet how affordable, Cape Syrah can be. This comes from plantations out towards the west coast, and has the unmistakable smoky miasma of the Cape, but that's all beautifully jumbled up with violet scent and rich loganberry and blackberry fruit.

2004 The Red Mullet [by Pikes], Clare Valley, Pikes Vintners, South Australia, 14.5% ABV
Vin du Van, £6.99

Red Mullet by Pikes. Geddit? The wine is luckily good enough to overcome the pun, and is a liaison dangereuse of Italian and Spanish grapes that works. There's loads of fresh blackcurrant fruit and exciting scents – eucalyptus, thyme and rosemary – but you never quite lose sight of the stony, dusty dryness that is such a feature of Italian Sangiovese.

2004 Cabernet Sauvignon-Merlot-Shiraz, Skuttlebutt, Stella Bella Wines, Margaret River, Western Australia, 14% ABV
Great Northern Wine, The Wine Society and other independent retailers, £6.95

Cabernet Sauvignon Merlot Shiraz

Unusual mix of Bordeaux and Rhône grapes from cool Western Australia, but the Aussies'll mix anything with anything if they think it'll work, and here it does. In fact it's a much deeper, richer brew than Margaret River normally comes up with, a big juicy soup of red plum syrup, chocolate, caramel and dates with the savoury rub of leather and a scent of eucalyptus gum. Skuttlebutt means 'gossip', by the way.

2006 Carmenère, el Grano, Central Valley, Chile, 13.5% ABV
Green & Blue, £6.85

This is unashamedly Carmenère, unashamedly Chilean in style, though the label proudly announces that 'the wine is elaborated by D. Duveau, French oenologist from Bordeaux's school'. Perhaps we should be grateful that he didn't learn too much about Bordeaux ways, because they don't make reds with this juicy, deliciously drinkable balance between ripe blackcurrant and black plum fruit and an utterly pleasurable pepper, celery and soy savouriness in Bordeaux. This is Chile through and through.

2005 Ribera del Duero, Dominio de Nogara, Bodegas Valtravieso, Castilla y León, Spain, 14% ABV
Playford Ros, £6.79

Ribera del Duero is one of Spain's most famous and overpriced areas, but the crazily expensive wines are not necessarily the most enjoyable – they're too often simply wodges of ultra-ripe fruit and expensive oak.

This supposedly lesser style is much more fun. It is a *little* tannic, but the deep mulberry and blueberry fruit with the scent of violet floating above the glass is delicious, and once you partner it with food you won't notice the tannin.

2005 Cabernet Sauvignon-Carmenère Reserva, Viña Porta, Chile, 14% ABV
Threshers, £6.49 (3 for 2, £4.33)

These two grapes go well together, providing great chunks of powerful fruit flavours that complement each other really well. This is a big, direct red packed with black cherry and black plum fruit and good rich ripe texture that is pulled back into line by the dusty fumes of coal smoke.

2004 Chilean Carmenère Reserva, The Best, Colchagua Valley, Chile, 13.5% ABV
Morrisons, £6.49

Morrisons have done well here to locate an archetypal, no holds barred Carmenère. Really obvious dark blackcurrant and damson fruit, coffee beans and celery cooked in a soy sauce and chocolate stew, with the smoke from the brazier swirling overhead.

2005 Syrah, Vin de Pays d'Oc, Camplazens, Château Camplazens, Languedoc-Roussillon, France, 13% ABV
Majestic, £6.49

This is such good stuff at such a fair price, I just think – why can't more people do this? French wines would leap out of the doldrums if there were more great value, great flavour reds like this. It's absolutely pinging with the classic flavours of the Syrah grape – a swoony violet scent, just a hint of smoke and a broad sweep of rich but dry damson and blackberry fruit.

2004 Cabernet Sauvignon, Co-op's Reserve, Coonawarra, South Australia, 13.5% ABV
Co-op, £5.99

Good, slightly lean, but very tasty Aussie Cabernet. Coonawarra is one of the coolest parts of South Australia, and this has lots of flavour without sporting a particularly dense texture. But that's good cool-climate style and neatly matches the blackcurrant fruit, the leafy scent softened by a touch of toffee syrup, then dried out and stood to attention by some earthy tar and the welcome rasp of pepper.

2004 Costers del Segre Crianza, Raimat Abadia, Cataluña, Spain, 13% ABV
Oddbins, £5.99

Raimat's wines are made in some of the most inhospitable areas in all of Spain. It took them literally generations to prepare the land to successfully grow decent grapes. But now they're doing a really good job of making bright modern wines in what is effectively a saltpan desert! This has full, grainy, but ripe red plum fruit just teetering on the richness of black, an attractive rasp of herbs and a surprising suggestion of apple blossom.

2006 Merlot, Don Cayetano, Colchagua Valley, Chile, 13.5% ABV
Laithwaites, £5.99

Good example of a Chilean red that says it's Merlot on the label, but in fact is much improved by the addition of Carmenère. This has big, powerful black plum verging on blackcurrant fruit with a little sour cherry, some pastry softness and good soy and celery savouriness. You wouldn't get all that without some help from the Carmenère.

2006 Pinot Noir, Cono Sur, Central Valley, Chile, 14% ABV
Widely available, £5.99

Cono Sur is probably the best-known affordable Pinot Noir in the world. It's always been enjoyable, sometimes very good, and this is the best one yet. It's a beautiful rich mixture of ripe strawberries in syrup and ripe Rosa plums drizzled with a little honey. But there are herbs and tannin too, to keep it from cloying. Lovely, mellow, lush but dry red.

2004 Syrah, Finca Antigua, La Mancha, Spain, 14.5% ABV
Majestic, £5.99

Leave this alone if you're of a fragile disposition. This is a big beast, it'll coat your teeth with dark stains and rough up your tonsils with fur – but it's sufficiently rich and ripe that come the winter it'll seem like the perfect red. Syrah doesn't usually grow in La Mancha, south of Madrid, but it seems to work, so long as you're after a bubbling cauldron of black plums and dates, smoky beef stock strewn with herbs, and a certain rich creaminess on the point of curdling under the assault of the plum skins' acidity.

2004 Touriga Nacional, Finest, Quinta da Fonte Bela, Estremadura, Portugal, 13.5% ABV
Tesco, £5.99

Year by year this is one of Tesco's most interesting and most consistent reds. Bulging with a personality that could only come from Portugal and its raft of indigenous grapes, this is a fascinating resiny mix of eucalyptus and lime, blackcurrant and cherry cake. There's some tannic roughness too, but with all that flavour the wine probably needs it.

2005 Californian Zinfandel, The Best, California, USA, 14.5% ABV
Morrisons, £5.99

Budget-priced Zinfandel is pretty hard to find – as a red wine, that is: the high street's shelves are awash with the sweet pink variety. So Morrisons have done well to find this big solid red Zin that tastes exactly as it should: blackberry jam fruit, a pervading scent of Virginia tobacco (unsmoked) and a good wodge of honey toffee texture.

2006 The Society's Chilean Pinot Noir (Viña Leyda), Leyda Valley, Chile, 14% ABV
The Wine Society, £5.95

Leyda is a new, super-cool, windy, foggy – I'm not selling this very well – vineyard area on Chile's coast. Its first releases have rocked the wine world: no one thought Chile could make really good Sauvignon or Pinot Noir. She can. In Leyda! Try this one. Almost syrupy rich, strawberry syrup coating smoky hazelnuts, scented by herbs and toughened up just a little with mineral dust. Pinot Noir is difficult to do cheaply. Or it was, until Leyda came along.

2005 Cabernet Sauvignon-Carignan, Equality by Las Lomas/Fairtrade, Maule Valley, Chile, 14% ABV
Morrisons, £5.79

Serious stuff – from a wild dry valley – pinging pure blackcurrant and eucalyptus with its focus smudged and its clarity fuddled by the addition of old Carignan. The result is a lovely drink: powerful Cabernet scent and fruit, broadened and rubbed with rock dust and the typical scratchy acidity and tannin of Carignan.

AROUND £5

For a lot of us a fiver seems a pretty fair price to pay for a bottle of wine. The retailers know this. They pack the £4.99 price point. Sometimes a wine's price stays there for years. What about inflation? What about duty increases, or difficult harvest conditions? The retailer doesn't care. The cost is relentlessly passed back to the producer, who either sees his or her profit dwindle, or who has to cut corners to make the price, and quality subtly subsides. Some retailers – just a few – don't do the £4.99 price point and they let their prices drift up when need be. So I've made a big effort to seek out the high streets' best and most reliable wines at around a fiver. And if it's a little bit more, well, that's because it's worth it.

- In this section you'll find whites first, then reds.

- My favourite white at this price is Peter Lehmann's Semillon, so I've put it first; after that I've put wines of similar style together, starting light and fresh, then getting zestier, and ending up with some softer and more aromatic examples.

- Red wines are also arranged by style, beginning with my top red, a juicy, raspberryish Saumur from the Loire Valley, and ending with a powerful beast from Spain.

WHITE WINE

2005 Semillon, Peter Lehmann, Barossa Valley, South Australia, 11.5% ABV
Tesco, £5.49

What a joy to see Peter Lehmann appearing more in our high streets once again: he is Australia's past master at giving value to his customers by dint of fair prices and fabulous flavours. And these flavours are untamed. If you're faint of heart and fearsome of new experiences, leave this wine alone. But if you like the sound of a bone-dry wine that is almost rocky in its seriousness, and yet which combines the scent of fresh leather with the richness of orange custard, the crunchiness of apple flesh and the searing essential oil acidity of lemon zest to choke the unwary – this is a must.

2006 Pinot Gris, Finca Las Higueras, Lurton, Mendoza, Argentina, 13% ABV
Waitrose, £5.55

The Lurtons are whizz-kid entrepreneurs and winemakers from Bordeaux in France, but they make extremely good wine all over the world. They've planted a vineyard in Argentina, high up towards the Andes, where they make Pinot Gris with real flavour – unlike a lot of the hyper-dilute examples we're being offered from Italy under the disturbingly trendy Pinot Grigio tag. This would do just as well for a light lunch white, but it has taste – full, ripe, redolent of pears, flavoured with apple, coated in cream.

2006 La Basca Uvas Blancas, Vino de la Tierra de Castilla y León, Spain, 13% ABV
Marks & Spencer, £5.49

Telmo Rodríguez is one of Spain's hottest young winemakers, and it's fantastic to see M&S hitching up with guys of such talent. What he's done here is to take the Verdejo and Viura grapes – both very dry, veering on the neutral in style – and create a dry wine full of sharp fruit – green nettle and grapefruit – spanking fresh and smelling of bananas and pears, and to counter its weight in the mouth, roughed up by the dryness of riverbed pebbles.

2006 Torrontés, Norton, Mendoza, Argentina, 12.5% ABV
Oddbins, £4.99

Most of Mendoza is too hot to make really fragrant Torrontés (you need the high mountain valleys) but I visited Norton's Torrontés vineyards with the guy who farms them and though they were within spitting distance of the heat-seeking Malbecs, he swore they made lovely wine. And they do. Classic, unashamed Torrontés: grape flesh richness sharpened by grapefruit, then wrapped in pastry, scythed apart by pungent lime zest and leaving a lingering aroma of lemon blossom.

2006 Sauvignon Blanc, Excelsior Estate, Robertson, South Africa, 12.5% ABV
Waitrose, £4.99

South Africa is making a lot of good Sauvignon Blanc nowadays and there are few better places to grow it than Robertson, with its limestone soils (which Sauvignon

and Chardonnay love) and cool breezes winding up the Breede River Valley. Add to this the fact that the Excelsior Estate is biodynamically farmed and I'm not surprised at the green apple peel and nettle leaf freshness of this wine, though it's a little softer than many Cape Sauvignons.

2006 Rueda, Casa del Sol, Sauvignon Blanc-Verdejo, Agricola Castellana, Castilla y León, Spain, 13% ABV
Co-op, £4.99

Rueda has the great ability to seem quite fat and soft, yet to be suffused with green sharp flavours. Maybe it's the paradox of its origins – a parched high plain of gaunt pebbly earth, boiled by day, frozen by night. This is quite full, with some soft cream and nut texture, but the character of the wine is green peel, green flesh and coffee bean flavour, tautened by bleached stones.

2005 Riesling, Eaglehawk, Wolf Blass, South Eastern Australia, 11.5% ABV
Sainsbury's, £5.49

Wolf Blass is a massive operation and most of its wines at this price level are entirely unmemorable. But this shows they *can* do the business if they want to. This is delightful dry Riesling, with good apple fruit, lashings of lemon zest and lemon juice acidity and a softness like leathery cream. It's a little mellower than some Aussie Rieslings but at £5.49 it might persuade an uncertain British public into trying Riesling wine. Riesling, by the way, is often the best of the Big Brands' offerings: Jacob's Creek is good too.

2006 Ribatejo, Portal da Águia, Portugal, 12.5% ABV
Oddbins, £4.99

Portugal isn't just about reds – it does good, individual whites as well and, in the main, from grape varieties unheard of anywhere else. This time it's the Arinto and the Fernão Pires and they make a pretty good pair, with all the come-hither being provided by white peach, melon and pear flesh juiciness, and a slight note of adult caution provided by zesty grapefruit pith and a streak of minerality like a shining rapier blade.

2006 Chardonnay-Verdelho-Semillon, Stickleback White, Heartland Wines, South Australia, 12.5% ABV
The Wine Society, £5.25

The description 'fresh, crisp, zesty' is not one I would normally apply to Australian Chardonnay. But this is made by the cutting edge Heartland operation, and when they promise you something, they deliver. What the winemaker has done here is to mix the plump Chardonnay with the acid Verdelho and the lean Semillon, pick all the grapes early so that the alcohol level is only 12.5%, and not let his precious liquid anywhere near an oak barrel. And it works. Green apple crunchiness is the most obvious flavour, fleshed out with a glyceriney fullness and a waft of smoky yeast softness. Fresh, crisp, zesty? Pretty much.

2005 The Society's Chilean Chardonnay (Viña Concha y Toro), Casablanca Valley, Chile, 13.5% ABV
The Wine Society, £5.50

The Wine Society used to favour Chardonnays which were good, but erred slightly on the tweed and old school tie side of things. This is much more modern, positively scented and, dare I say it, ever so slightly feminine – mixing

melon and honey and mineral dryness with a scent that's like a floral and nut-based face cream. Now, which is it? Is it L'Oreal, or Caudalie, or Dior …?

2006 Viognier, La Baume, Winemaker's Selection, Languedoc-Roussillon, France, 13.5% ABV
Waitrose, £4.99

This has such a lovely rich spicy quality I thought it had been aged in new oak barrels. But then I thought, not at a price tag of £4.99 – and so I checked. No oak. Pure fruit. This exotic heady spice comes from the grape, the same grapes that give fruit simply oozing with lush apricot juice, the same grapes that provide beguiling floral scent and resinous zesty grapefruit to keep everything fresh.

2006 Viognier, Trivento, Mendoza, Argentina, 13.5% ABV
Waitrose, £4.99

This is made in Argentina by Chile's biggest wine producer, Concha y Toro. They've planted hundreds of acres in Argentina's best valleys, especially the cool Tupungato – and cool is of enormous importance in making good whites in the generally pretty torrid Argentine. This is delightful, fresh, bright, not at all complicated but exceedingly drinkable, with scented apricot fruit and a mouthwatering nip of acidity.

RED WINE

2006 Saumur Rouge, Les Nivières (Cave de Saumur), Loire Valley, France, 13.5% ABV
Waitrose, £4.99

Oh, what a wine for this price. It's throbbing with personality, with an unmistakable sense of place, of a vineyard, of great grapes grown just there and nowhere else. These are Cabernet Franc grapes grown on the pale, crumbly soils of Saumur, more a white wine destination, but brilliant for red. Cabernet Franc is a real star of the Loire Valley, especially when the wine can sing pure and crystalline with no oak aging. Here, there's not a whiff of oak, just luscious, deep, ripe raspberry and blackcurrant fruit and a chalky, pebbly tide running through the wine as though the vineyard can't bear to be parted from its fruit.

nv Garnacha Tinto, Navarra, Spain, 14% ABV
Threshers, £4.99 (3 for 2, £3.33)

Garnacha is by far the best grape variety to make Spain's red gluggers. This isn't supposed to be subtle – and it isn't. Garnacha makes wine for the heart and the belly, not the brain – although it'll fuddle the brain quicker than most. And at its best it's juicy, stony, herb-strewn, full of squashy strawberry and rough-cut red plum fruit – and full of the scent of alcohol. For the right kind of party, this is the juice.

2006 Pinot Noir (Morandé), Casablanca Valley, Chile, 14% ABV
Marks & Spencer, £4.99

M&S do seem to have a knack of sniffing out Chilean Pinot Noir. This is their basic one, but it's got a fair bit of class – that elusive, gentle, rich strawberry fruit that so many producers try to create and fail, just a touch of tannic toughness and pleasantly integrated smoky oak. For £4.99? That'll do nicely.

2006 Tempranillo-Syrah, Palacio del Marqués, Castilla-La Mancha, Spain, 14.5% ABV
Marks & Spencer, £4.49

La Mancha used to be dismissed as an arid high plateau incapable of producing anything but drabbest plonk. But the modern wine world is transforming these high areas and, helped as here by New World gurus like the Australian Peter Bright, exciting, affordable wines are popping up. This is excellent, juicy, bright-eyed stuff, smelling as fresh as apples and pears, and tasting of ripe red plums and strawberry dust.

2006 Cabernet Sauvignon-Carmenère, Old Vines, Doña Dominga, Viña Casa Silva, Colchagua Valley, Chile, 13.5% ABV
Oddbins, £5.49

These two grapes mix well. Both have a core of ripe blackcurrant to feed off, and two's better than one. What Carmenère brings is a burly savoury influence that seasons the blackcurrant with soy sauce, celery and pepper. When the balance is right, the wine is powerful and delicious.

2006 Carmenère, Los Robles Fairtrade, Curicó Valley, Chile, 13% ABV
Asda, Sainsbury's, Waitrose, £4.99

This gladdens the heart. Fairtrade Carmenère has become a big hit since it arrived a few years ago and it now sells shedloads. It would have been easy for

the producers – especially with Fairtrade to bank on for our goodwill – to dilute the quality. But, God bless 'em, they haven't. In fact, this is the best Fairtrade Carmenère yet – bellowing its wonderful, unique Carmenère flavours of raw ripe blackcurrant fruit assaulted in thrilling cacophony by white pepper and celery, parsley, coriander and soy. Carmenère at its naked best. And by the way, the money you spend really does do good. I've been there. I've seen.

2006 Merlot, Otra Vida, Mendoza, Argentina, 13.5% ABV
Waitrose, £4.99

Merlot isn't easy to grow in the warm parts of Mendoza – it ripens very quickly and much prefers cool conditions. But they've made a good job of this – quite a rich texture just nipped by tannin, and attractive red plum fruit washed over with cream.

2006 Chilean Merlot, SO Organic, Central Valley, Chile, 13.5% ABV
Sainsbury's, £4.99

This is excellent stuff, every vintage, and the more we buy, the more we persuade the Chileans that they could do organic in most of their country if they set their minds to it. This is dark, rich, brooding wine, but not sullen, a splat of tannin is brushed aside by powerful blackcurrant and black plum fruit wreathed in smoke and splashed with soy sauce.

2005 The Society's Chilean Merlot (Viña Concha y Toro), Rapel Valley, Chile, 14% ABV
The Wine Society, £5.50

I thought this was a bit oaky when I first opened it, but I went back to the bottle an hour later and all it needed was some air. It's quite a chunky beast, and does have a certain growl of coal smoke bitterness about it, but that actually provides rather a good counterpoint for the rich blackcurrant juice and eucalyptus scent that are what the wine's all about.

2005 Quinta de Bons-Ventos, Casa Santos Lima, Estremadura, Portugal, 12.5% ABV
Oddbins, £4.99

Now this is the kind of stuff that could really give Portugal a good name. Portugal has so many wonderful grape varieties, so many good vineyards, so many fine winemakers – yet the wines still don't catch fire in the UK. Well, try this one and, if you like it, try some others. It's made from four totally Portuguese grape varieties. You really want to know? OK: Castelão (very good), Camarate (very good), Tinta Miuda (very good) and Touriga Nacional (very, very good). And they meld together here into a lovely, deep, out-of-focus fuzz of cherry cake, cherry syrup, strawberries and a lick of honey, that is absolutely delightful. They do make wines that are very much in focus, too. But at £4.99, and after a glass or two, I kind of like the out of focus.

2006 Nerello Mascalese, Sicily, Italy, 13% ABV
Marks & Spencer, £4.49

M&S have been doing some good work in Italy, particularly in the south, and I'm delighted to see more and more of the local grapes popping up over here. This is delightful, characterful wine, very much its own style, being soft in texture but reasonably dense, with red bitter cherry fruit that isn't raw, in fact is slightly jellyish, and an undertow of lava, basalt and hillside herbs.

2006 Carignan, Vin de Pays des Coteaux de Peyriac, Domaine La Tour Boisée, Languedoc-Roussillon, France, 13.8% ABV
Waterloo Wine, £4.99

Almost inky deep, yet no sign of the ripe richness of blackcurrants, blackberries or damsons. Whatever fruit there is is red – concentrated red plum, red cherry, cranberry – and it's roughened up by the rasp of unripe apple skins and scratched with the bitterness of stone. Yet somehow this beetle-browed lout manages a toffee sweet finish. And somehow, I like it.

2006 Carignan, La Différence, Vin de Pays des Côtes Catalanes, Languedoc-Roussillon, France, 13.5% ABV
Co-op, Sainsbury's, £4.99

This comes from the very heart of La France Sauvage, and uses as its grape the grand old man of savagery, the variety all the authorities and modernists want to pull out for being too coarse, too rustic – the Carignan. Luckily there's still loads of old Carignan planted away from the mainstream in France and Spain, producing wild grog like this: a dark dense stew of red fruit and raisins, herbs and leather, the roughness of rocks, the odour of animals, alive, then roasted on the fire. It's pretty fierce but a) you could age it for five to ten years, and b) some like it fierce – and it is called La Différence, for goodness sake.

2004 Shiraz Reserve, First Flight, South Eastern Australia, 13.5% ABV
Somerfield, £4.99

The Somerfield wine buyer got tired of the dull quality of Australian commercial Shiraz she was being offered, so she flew off to blend her own. And she did good. This is a very pleasant mix of smoky black plum with just a touch of blackcurrant, a whiff of coal dust and the freshening nip of citrus acid.

2006 Australian Shiraz (Yalumba), 13.5% ABV
Marks & Spencer, £4.99

I'm delighted to see Yalumba starting to appear more and more in our high streets. It's people like Rob Hill-Smith of Yalumba and Peter Lehmann (see page 82) who are the heart of Australian wine: they understand value and customer satisfaction like no others. This Shiraz is exactly what a £4.99 Shiraz should be – and then a bit – bursting out with rich, ripe red cherry, loganberry and sweet plum fruit, fattened up with smoky chocolate, scattered with herbs, yet it remains juicy, balanced and eminently drinkable. There used to be lots of commercial Shiraz like this. There isn't now. But at least we still have Yalumba.

2004 Shiraz Reserve, The Boulders, California, USA, 13.5% ABV
Co-op, £5.49

I wish we got more affordable tasty Californian wine like this in the UK. So much stuff in this price area is so flat and lifeless. But The Boulders delivers – and then some. It's full, it's ripe, it's rich – hell, it's unctuous – but it's not sweet and it's not sugared up. It's rich with clotted cream, it's rich with black plums and prunes and dates, but it's also chilled down by a stony dryness and the texture is soft like cold beeswax, not grape stew.

2005 Shiraz, Wildcard, Peter Lehmann, South Australia, 14.5% ABV
Co-op, £4.99

Here's the mighty Peter Lehmann trying to seduce us back to Australian Shiraz by offering irresistible flavour at a fair price. Wildcard is Lehmann's lightest Shiraz, yet it still has classic smoky blackberry sauce richness, a blackness of chocolate and prunes seasoned with herbs and fresh leather. Thanks, Peter, keep it up.

2006 Toro, Finca Sobreño, Castilla y León, Spain, 14.5% ABV
Co-op, £4.99

Toro's always powerful stuff: it has a brutal quality of tannic bitterness and aggression. But it balances that with great gobs of solid, rough-hewn fruit. Absolutely *not* the red to drink as an aperitif. Absolutely *the* wine for a great slab of grilled steak. This one smells surprisingly fresh – pear and plum flesh and some leafy greenness too – but the flavour of the wine is meaty, dense, rattled by stones, coiled in black plum syrup and savoury cream.

CHEAP AND CHEERFUL

We used to do a whole section of wines at £2.99. But then I began to think, why? There *is* still some decent grog to be had below £3, but you just know the producer is being screwed down to that price point and I didn't feel good any more about devoting much time to such wines. Anyway, do you really need any help to buy the cheapest plonk in the shop? I want you to trade up. I'd like to lead you up to a fiver and beyond, but if I can at least persuade you up to four quid or so, there's some pleasant stuff to be had – and here it is.

- In this section you'll find whites first, then reds.

- My first choice at this price is a peach of an Aussie Chardonnay; after that I've grouped wines from light and lemony to aromatic and floral.

- My top red-wine bargain is a wonderfully fresh French red from the Rhône Valley; at this price you should find lots of juicy young gluggers, as well as food-friendly wines from southern France – and these are some of my current favourites.

WHITE WINE

2005 Chardonnay Reserve, Bushland (Hope Estate), Hunter Valley, New South Wales, Australia, 13% ABV
Aldi, £3.99

Aldi introduced this last year to rave reviews. This is the new vintage and it's just as good. Real, serious, deep Chardonnay from one of Australia's most expensive regions – and check the price! Maybe it's because this style of Chardonnay has gone out of fashion a bit. Well, I can understand. It's not sleek and modern, but it's packed with fat peach fruit and nut syrup, it's got a savoury leather scent and a smooth waxy texture. For £3.99? Take a punt.

2005 Verdicchio dei Castelli di Jesi Classico, Moncaro, Marche, Italy, 12.5% ABV
Waitrose, £3.99

Good, full, direct, tasty Italian white. It hasn't got all kinds of complex flavours – very few Italian whites have – but you do get that fluffy soft flesh of a ripe apple and the sharp crunch of the peel, a hint of lemon and a smear of honeyed cream.

2006 Hungarian Pinot Grigio (Hilltop Neszmély), 12.5% ABV
Marks & Spencer, £4.29

Hungarian Pinot Gris is fantastically good. Some traditions have it that the grape variety comes from there, so we should pay these Danube delights a bit more respect. This isn't quite dry, and has an utterly charming flavour of white and pink apple flesh, honeydew melon and the restrained zesty acidity of boiled lemons.

2006 Pinot Grigio, Recas, Romania, 12.5% ABV
Wines of Westhorpe, £3.93

If only Pinot Grigios at £2 more had half as much character as this. Romania has been growing Pinot Grigio for ever and her wines are packed with personality – banana and pear, raw apple and a sharp squirt of lemon. It makes for an excellent white. I hope someone buys it.

2006 Cuvée Pecheur, Vin de Pays du Comté Tolosan, South-West France, 11.5% ABV
Waitrose, £3.49

The Gascony region of South-West France traditionally grew grapes to make Armagnac brandy. As demand for that fell away, they've started turning the acid, green grapes into splendidly refreshing, tart, sharp but fruity dry white wines. This is spitting with green leaf and apple peel venom. If you like this style – it's like a tangy Sauvignon in all but name – South-West France offers you the world's best value.

2006 Cuvée de Richard (white), Vin de Pays du Comté Tolosan, South-West France, 11.5% ABV
Majestic, £3.19

All the good guys turn up in Gascony for their French house white. This is snappy, sharp, but not raw, with lots of grapefruit zest, apple peel and fresh citrus juice acidity.

2006 Vin de Pays du Gers (white), South-West France, 11.5% ABV
Marks & Spencer, £3.49

Another nice snappy fresh dry white from South-West France. This is relatively soft, but that doesn't get in the way of lemon pith zing, green apple fruit and a hint of herbs and peppercorn. Tesco also has a version, at £2.99.

2006 Bordeaux, Chateaux's Selection (Benoit Calvet), Sauvignon-Semillon, Bordeaux, France, 12% ABV
Aldi, £3.29

Good, citrous dry white wine at a very good price. Lemon and grapefruit zest blending cheerily with apple and melon fruit and a hint of nutty yeast to soften it.

2006 Matra Springs, Gyöngyös, Hungary, 11% ABV
Waitrose, £3.99

The best value dry aromatic white on the market. A mixture of Pinot Gris and Leányka is topped off with the heady, grapy Muscat Ottonel, and the result is this delightful, spicy, floral white mixing lemon zest and grapefruit flower with a crunchy Muscat fruit.

RED WINE

2006 Vin de Pays de l'Ardèche Gamay, Rhône Valley, France, 12% ABV
Marks & Spencer, £3.49

Fresh, fresh, fresh. You can't get red wine fresher than this. Country fresh, meadow fresh, mountain fresh, the ultimate juicy glugger – what Beaujolais ought to deliver, yet so rarely does. It's the same grape as Beaujolais – Gamay – and they've grown it in the hills west of the Rhône Valley for ages. I've always been expecting it to catch on in Britain, and it never does. Well, slurp some of this down and see if I'm right, see if you drool for its peach and strawberry fruit and its creamy summer earth. Then remind yourself it only costs £3.49 and buy six.

2006 Bonarda, Dios del Sol, Mendoza, Argentina, 12.5% ABV
Somerfield, £3.99

Bonarda is Argentina's highly effective workhorse grape. This red is a solid chunky red fruit soup with a flicker of typical Bonarda wild strawberry perfume. I wish we saw more Bonarda here. It should be Argentina's answer to Beaujolais.

2006 Fruits of France Grenache, Vin de Pays d'Oc, Languedoc-Roussillon, France, 14.5% ABV
Waitrose, £3.99

The Grenache grape (known as Garnacha in Spain) gives lovely, juicy, rather alcoholic reds and pinks all around the western Mediterranean – and they're hardly ever expensive. This is spot-on basic red, with loads of straight-up plum and strawberry fruit, a slap of herbs, and a dash of refreshing acidity. Go for it.

2005 Côtes du Ventoux, La Rectorie, Rhône Valley, France, 13% ABV
Majestic, Waitrose, £3.99

Good, fresh, light red with attractive bright dry plum and strawberry fruit, just a touch of tannin and some fresh herb scent.

2006 Trinacria Rosso, Sicily, Italy, 11% ABV
Waitrose, £3.49

Lovely mild red made from a bunch of local grape varieties. It's light, easygoing, tasting of apples, strawberries and honey. Not a hard edge in sight.

2005 Cabernet Sauvignon, La Finca, Finca La Celia, Mendoza, Argentina, 13.5% ABV
Co-op, £3.99

Finca La Celia is a good operation, so the Co-op has done well to get this wine at £3.99. It's a good meaty red, but the meat is matched by some floral scent, creamy texture and good blackberry fruit.

2006 Carignan Old Vines, Vin de Pays de l'Aude, Le Sanglier de la Montagne, Caves du Mont Tauch, Languedoc-Roussillon, France, 12.5% ABV
Booths, £3.49

'The wild boar of the mountain' is what the locals have labelled this wine. And they do have legions of wild boar in the hills. This rough and ready red would be great for the marinade, the sauce, and for drinking in great flagons with the beast. It's not that concentrated, but it has really good rugged raw apple and cherry fruit, slapped with a bit of tannic bite, but soothed with rosehip scent and herbs of the mountain slopes.

2006 Cuvée de Richard (red), Vin de Pays de l'Aude, Languedoc-Roussillon, France, 12% ABV
Majestic, £3.19

Rough-cut, chunky, solid but juicy red. Absolutely no frills, but a good example of what basic southern French red should be.

2006 Côtes du Rhône (Celliers des Dauphins), Rhône Valley, France, 14.5% ABV
Marks & Spencer, £3.99

Dead straight, full-bodied stony red wine, ripe with the Rhône Valley sun and rough-rubbed by the raw rocky landscape. A little Syrah in the blend adds some extra stewy fruit.

nv Corbières, Reserve des Vignerons, Caves du Mont Tauch, Languedoc-Roussillon, France, 12.5% ABV
Somerfield, £3.49

The Mont Tauch winery is set in some of the wilder landscapes of southern France, so I'm delighted when the reds reflect their mountain origins. This is a stony red, with ripe red plum fruit and a hillside scent of bayleaf mixed with angostura.

ROSÉ WINES

I'm not going to give you complicated, poetic tasting notes about the pink wines, because any half-decent rosé shouldn't have anything complicated to write about. It should sport a come-hither bright fresh colour, a fresh, inviting aroma and a happy party and picnic easygoing flavour, whether bone dry or not quite. These are good-time gluggers. And they're becoming very popular. Last year we noted a huge increase in their popularity. This year supermarkets report pink sales shooting ahead again, often up 50 per cent. So here are the pick of the pinks.

- My favourite rosé this year also happens to be the most expensive and therefore the first in this section; after that I've listed wines in descending price order.

2005 Zweigelt, Langenloiser Rosé, Trocken, Bründlmayer, Kamptal, Austria, 12% ABV
Bacchus, Raeburn, Sommelier, £9.99

I'm tempted to say that this is a pink you must take seriously. It's from the excellent Zweigelt grape grown in excellent vineyards by one of Austria's greatest winemakers; he'd say, chill it down. Drink it. End of story. But I have to tell you, it's got a fabulous flavour of apple flesh and strawberry, radishes and a spray of white pepper.

2006 Chapel Down English rosé, 11.5% ABV
Waitrose, £8.99

This is a mix of white grapes and red – especially new red varieties Rondo and Regent, which give great flavour and colour even under the pale English sun. Well, it isn't pale any more, of course, but our reds still need a bit of help ripening. However, red grapes that aren't quite ripe can make smashing rosé – and this has a lovely smoky apple flavour, a cream cheese texture tempered by summer earth and a gentle, ripe red fruit aftertaste.

2006 Côtes de Provence rosé, Château Saint Baillon, Provence, France, 12.5% ABV
Goedhuis & Co, £7.74

Côtes de Provence pinks are some of the most expensive in France, and with a captive audience dying of thirst on the local beaches every summer, willing to suck up any old stuff at a silly price, we don't see much Provence rosé over here. But this one's good – fleshy for Provence, but still dry, with mildly squashy apple fruit and a hint of rich date ripeness.

2005 Costières de Nîmes rosé, Cuvée Prestige, Château Roubaud, Rhône Valley, France, 13% ABV Yapp Brothers, £7.60

The Rhône Valley makes a lot of really nice rosé. Some of the best comes from the far south, where the vineyards are stony and warm – and this wine is deep, stony, mouthfilling with glycerine texture and full of apple and strawberry fruit.

2006 Ribera del Duero rosado, El Quintanal, Castilla y León, Spain, 13% ABV Oddbins, £7.29

Ribera del Duero makes some of the most serious, sought-after red wine in Spain. But that doesn't stop them wanting a drop of something more light-hearted – this is fresh, creamy and full flavoured, but chill it down and it does the trick.

2006 Costières de Nîmes Rosé, Château Guiot, Rhône Valley, France, 13.5% ABV Majestic, £6.24

Powerful, rumbustious pink – loads of strawberry but also some windfall apples, syrup richness damped down with stony dry weight, and a welcome hint of herbs.

2006 Slowine Rosé, South Africa, 13% ABV Butlers, Flagship, Christopher Piper Wines, £5.99

The whole point about the Slowine, Slow Food, slow life movement is that you take time out to savour all the experiences that our existence offers us. I suppose you *could* drink this delightful pink slowly, with its strawberry and plum fruit ripeness, its apple acidity and undertow of pebbles and iron, but why not drink it fast and cold while slowly contemplating the meaning of life?

2006 Cabernet Sauvignon Rosé, San Medín, Miguel Torres, Curicó Valley, Chile, 13.5% ABV
Waitrose, £5.99

Great grape, great winemaker – and this wine's for drinking, not philosophizing. Even so, for a rosé, it's bulging, it's rippling with blackcurrant fruit and strawberry syrup. Rich but balanced and good. Very tasty.

2006 Marques de Rojas Rosado, Bodegas Piqueras, Almansa, Castilla-La Mancha, Spain, 13.5% ABV
Averys, £5.99

It gets pretty hot in Almansa, inland from Alicante, and I suspect the Syrah grape struggles a bit under the relentless sun. But it still produces a pretty tasty pink – creamy in style, full in texture, but with quite enough pear, apple and strawberry fruit to make it an enjoyable drink.

2006 Rioja Rosado, Gran Familia, Bodegas Castillo de Fuenmayor, Rioja, Spain, 12% ABV
Tesco, £4.99

Rioja has been making really tasty pinks for as long as I can remember, but everyone dismisses them in the rush for red. Not me. This is full of apple and strawberry fruit topped off with cream, and has a very lulling waxy texture too.

2006 Le Froglet Rosé, Vin de Pays d'Oc, Languedoc-Roussillon, France, 12% ABV
Marks & Spencer, £4.99

Froglet. How sweet. Surely this can't be the French poking mild fun at themselves? Well, Froglet turns out to be a very nice, easy pink wine with gentle pear, apple and strawberry fruit – a swig of this and they'll find it a lot easier to laugh at themselves.

nv Navarra Rosado, Torre Beratxa, Navarra, Spain, 13.5% ABV
Threshers, £4.99 (3 for 2, £3.33)

Ah, Spain is so good at this style. The Garnacha grape makes marvellous, herb-strewn chunky reds, but also fresh, bright, full-flavoured yet fresh pinks, packed with apple and pear and strawberry fruit that cry out for chilling and knocking back.

2006 Navarra Rosado, Malumbres, Bodegas Vicente Malumbres, Navarra, Spain, 13.5% ABV
The Wine Society, £4.95

The Garnacha grape makes ace rosé: this one's enjoyable, bright, fresh, a mellow mix of strawberry and apple and cream, with just a little stony roughness.

2006 Tempranillo rose, Tierra Sana (organically grown grapes), La Mancha, Spain, 13% ABV
Co-op, £3.99

This tops the list for flavour per quid. It does have the usual apple and strawberry fruit, mellowed by cream and swirled with a little summer dust, but it also has an extra layer of fruit, of pear and melon, and a texture softened with wax.

2006 Utiel-Requena rosado, Viña Decana, Valencia, Spain, 12.5% ABV
Aldi, £2.99

Another well-made pink from a baking hot area, this time inland from Valencia. You can taste a bit of rich date ripeness, which tells you the sun was really beating down, but they've managed to keep some bright strawberry fruit and some quite sharp apple peel acidity to nip your tonsils.

Keeping it light

We're becoming increasingly disenchanted with high-alcohol wines. So, increasingly, I'm checking the alcohol content of the wines I recommend. Here are my suggestions for drinks with fab flavours, that won't leave you fuzzy-headed the next morning.

More and more wines seem to be hitting our shores at 14%, 15% – we even had a wine in a tasting here recently that topped 16%. A red table wine! How can you enjoy that as a jolly beverage to knock back with your lamb chops: you'll be asleep or drunk before you've got the meat off the barbie.

Now, some wines have traditionally been high alcohol, and wear their strength well, but there are far too many wines that – less than a decade ago – used to perform at 11.5 to 12.5% alcohol and which are now adding at least a degree – and often more – to their strength, seemingly in an effort to ape the ripe round flavours of the New World. Thank goodness there are still a significant number showing more restraint.

At 12.5% there are lots of wines, particularly from cooler parts of France – most Beaujolais is 12–12.5% – northern Italy, where the most famous examples would be the Veneto reds Valpolicella and Bardolino and the white Soave, and from numerous parts of Eastern Europe, particularly Hungary.

But we've set the bar at 12%. This cuts out a lot of red wines; the slightly tart, refreshing white styles that sit easily at 12% can develop better flavour at a lower strength than most reds can. This exercise reminded us that Germany is full of fantastic Riesling wines as low as 7.5%. Muscadet is usually only 12%. Most supermarket house reds and whites are 11.5–12%. Western Australia whites are often 12%. And Champagne, of all things, is only 12%. Hallelujah.

White wine

- 2005 Atlantique, Vin de Pays des Côtes de Gascogne, Sauvignon Blanc-Gros Manseng, South-West France, £4.99, Co-op, 12% ABV

- 2005 Blanc de Morgex et de la Salle, Vini Estremi, Valle d'Aosta, Italy, £9.28, les Caves de Pyrene, 11.5% ABV (page 44)

- 2006 Bordeaux, Chateaux's Selection, Sauvignon-Semillon, Bordeaux, France, £3.29, Aldi, 12% ABV (page 98)

- 2003 Les 4 Cépages (Gros Manseng, Chardonnay, Sauvignon, Semillon), Vin de Pays des Côtes de Gascogne, Tariquet, Famille Grassa, South-West France, £8.99 (3 for 2 £5.99), Threshers, 12% ABV (page 46)

- 2005 Chablis, Domaine Billaud-Simon, Burgundy, France, £9.95, Wine Society, 12% ABV (page 26)

- 2005 Chablis, Vieilles Vignes, Domaine de Bieville, Burgundy, France, £10.69, Laithwaites, 12% ABV

- 2006 Chenin Blanc, Peter Lehmann, Barossa, South Australia, £5.99, Waitrose, 11.5% ABV

- 2006 Colombard-Sauvignon Blanc, La Biondina, Primo Estate, McLaren Vale, South Australia, £10.15, Philglas & Swiggot, 12% ABV (page 42)

- 2006 Cuvée Pecheur, Vin de Pays du Comté Tolosan, South-West France, £3.49, Waitrose, 11.5% ABV (page 97)

- 2006 Cuvée de Richard, Vin de Pays du Comté Tolosan, South-West France, £3.19, Majestic, 11.5% ABV (page 97)

- 2006 Dourthe No. 1, Bordeaux Sauvignon Blanc, France, £5.99, Waitrose, 12% ABV

- 2006 Matra Springs, Gyöngyös, Hungary, £3.99, Waitrose, 11% ABV (page 98)

- 2006 Muscadet Côtes de Grandlieu Sur Lie, Fief Guérin, Loire Valley, France, £5.35, Waitrose, 12% ABV

- 2006 Muscadet Sèvre at Maine Sur Lie, Le Moulin de Cossardieres, Loire Valley, France, £4.99, Marks & Spencer, 12% ABV

- 2006 Muscadet Sèvre et Maine, Domaine de la Tourmaline, Loire Valley, France, £5.49, Majestic, 12% ABV

- 2005 Oddbins Own White, Languedoc-Roussillon, France, £3.99, Oddbins, 12% ABV

- 2006 Domaine de Plantérieu, Vin de Pays des Côtes de Gascogne, South-West France, £4.29, Waitrose, 10.5% ABV

- 2006 Riesling, Tim Adams, Clare Valley, South Australia, £7.99, Tesco, 12% ABV (page 50)

- 2005 Riesling, Basserman-Jordan, Pfalz, Germany, £7.49, Waitrose, 11% ABV

- nv Riesling, The Best, Ewald Pfeiffer, Mosel-Saar-Ruwer, Germany, £5.99, Morrisons, 9% ABV

- 2005 Riesling, Blue Slate, Dr Loosen, Mosel, Germany, £7.99, Somerfield, 8.5% ABV
- 2005 Riesling, Eaglehawk, Wolf Blass, Australia, £5.49, Sainsbury's, 11.5% ABV (page 84)
- 2005 Riesling, Graffenreben, Alsace, France, £6.99, Waitrose, 12% ABV
- 2006 Riesling Kabinett, Ayler Kupp, Margarethenhof, Mosel, Germany, £5.99, Majestic, 9% ABV
- 2006 Riesling Kabinett, Graacher Himmelreich, Dr Loosen, Mosel, Germany, £9.99, Sainsbury's, 7.5% ABV
- 2005 Riesling Kabinett, Leitz Estate, Rüdesheim, Rheingau, Germany, £7.49, Tesco, 8.5% ABV
- 2004 Riesling Kabinett, Ürziger Würzgarten, Karl Erbes, Mosel, Germany, £6.99, Waitrose, 8% ABV
- 2005 Riesling, Rüdesheimer Berg Roseneck Old Vines, Leitz Estate, Rheingau, Germany, £17, Marks & Spencer, 8.5% ABV
- 2006 Riesling, Danny Schuster, Waipara, New Zealand, £7.05, les Caves de Pyrene, 10.5% ABV (page 54)
- 2006 Rioja, Gran Familia, Bodegas Castillo de Fuenmayor, Rioja, Spain, £4.99, Co-op, 12% ABV
- 2006 Sauvignon Blanc, Ormonde Cellars, Darling, South Africa, £6.99, Tesco, 12% ABV (page 55)
- 2006 Sauvignon Blanc, Oxford Landing, South Australia, £6.99, widely available, 11% ABV
- 2006 Sauvignon Blanc-Semillon, Harewood Estate, Denmark, Western Australia, £8.95, Great Western Wine, Noel Young, 12% ABV (page 47)
- 2006 Sauvignon Blanc-Semillon Reserve, Palandri Estate, Western Australia, £6.99, Co-op, 11.5% ABV
- 2006 Sauvignon Blanc-Semillon, Western Australia, £6.99, Sainsbury's Taste the Difference, 12% ABV
- 2001 Semillon, Mount Pleasant Elizabeth, McWilliam's, Hunter Valley, New South Wales, Australia, £9.99, Morrisons, 11% ABV (page 42)
- 2005 Semillon, Peter Lehmann, Barossa, South Australia, £5.49, Tesco, 11.5% ABV (page 82)
- 2000 Semillon Reserve, Peter Lehmann, Barossa, South Australia, £10.99, Portland, Vin du Vin, Noel Young, 11.5% ABV (page 20)
- 2006 Semillon-Sauvignon Blanc, Verse 1, Brookland Valley, Margaret River, Western Australia, £8.99, Oddbins, 12% ABV
- 2006 Soave (Organic), Veneto, Italy, £4.99, Marks & Spencer, 12% ABV
- 2006 Vin de Pays des Côtes de Gascogne, les Quatre Cépages (Colombard, Sauvignon, Ugni Blanc, Gros Manseng), Domaine de Pajot, South-West France, £4.79, Booths, Organic, 12% ABV

- 2006 Vin de Pays du Gers, South-West France, £3.49, Marks & Spencer, 11.5% ABV (page 98)
- 2006 Vin de Pays de l'Hérault, Moulin de Gassac, Mas de Daumas Gassac, Languedoc-Roussillon, France, £5.99, Averys, 12% ABV

Rosé wine

- 2006 Chapel Down rosé, England, £8.99, Waitrose, 11.5% ABV (page 104)
- 2005 Cheverny, Domaine Sauger, Loire Valley, France, £8.99, Flagship Wines, 12% ABV
- 2006 Le Froglet Rosé, Vin de Pays d'Oc, Languedoc, France, £4.99, Marks & Spencer, 12% ABV (page 106)
- 2005 Langenloiser Rosé, Zweigelt, Brundlmayer, Kamptal, Austria, £9.99, Raeburn Fine Wines, 12% ABV (page 104)
- 2006 Rioja Rosado, Gran Familia, Bodegas Castillo de Fuenmayor, Rioja, Spain, £4.99, Tesco, 12% ABV (page 106)

Red wine

- 2006 Beaujolais, Cuvée Terroir, Domaine Chatelus, Beaujolais, France, £7.35, Roger Harris Wines, 12% ABV (page 73)

- 2006 Cuvée Chasseur, Vin de Pays de l'Hérault, Languedoc-Roussillon, France, £3.49, Waitrose, 12% ABV
- 2006 Cuvée de Richard, Vin de Pays de l'Aude, Languedoc-Roussillon, France, £3.19, Majestic, 12% ABV (page 101)
- 2006 House Wine, Vin de Pays du Comté Tolosan, South-West France, £3.49, Marks & Spencer, 12% ABV
- 2004 Terrano,Carso, Zidarich, Friuli-Venezia Giulia, Italy, £17.55, les Caves de Pyrene, 11.5% (page 36)
- 2006 Trinacria Rosso, Sicily, Italy, £3.49, Waitrose, 11% ABV (page 100)
- 2006 Vieille Fontaine, Vin de Pays du Comté Tolosan, South-West France, £2.99, Tesco, 12% ABV
- 2006 Vin de Pays de l'Ardèche Gamay, Rhône Valley, France, £3.49, Marks & Spencer, 12% ABV (page 99)

FIZZ

These warm summers are really are making a difference to our drinking habits. Walk through a city park any time from April to October and there are dozens of groups of people laughing, chatting, picnicking – and drinking wine. In particular fizz. I asked one park-keeper what were the empties he picked up most. He grinned and said 'Champagne'. Well, some of it may have been sparkling wine, not true Champagne. But the message was clear – we love fizz, and the longer the sun stays out, the more we'll drink of it. I haven't included most of the big-brand Champagnes here because you can get better stuff for a tenner less – that tenner would have gone on their advertising and marketing budget, not on extra quality. And, as our winners show, you don't have to be drinking Champagne to get stunning Champagne flavours.

2002 Pelorus, Cloudy Bay, New Zealand
Majestic, Sainsbury's and independent retailers, £17–£19

Wonderful stuff. I've been praising the non-vintage Pelorus for years, often using it in blind tastings where it triumphantly routed much more expensive and famous names from Champagne itself. And I'd half-forgotten Pelorus make a vintage wine, too, which is even better. Pelorus is the sparkling wine of Cloudy Bay in New Zealand. Cloudy Bay is owned by the same bunch as Veuve Clicquot, Moët & Chandon, all that lot. So this is sort of down-under Veuve Clicquot. Well, I hope the French guys get hold of a few bottles, because this has more class than their Champagne offering, and it's way cheaper. It's fabulously creamy, it's pulsating with lively apple flesh and hazelnuts wrapped in soft yeast, and the bubbles foam and flirt around your tongue. You could age this for another five years and it would be even better – but it's fantastic now.

nv Jansz Rosé, Yalumba, Tasmania, Australia
Flagship, Oddbins, Oz Wines, Philglas & Swiggot, Selfridges, Noel Young, £9.99

Jansz is a Tasmanian outfit, originally started by Champagne house Louis Roederer and now owned by Aussie star family firm Yalumba. I use the non-vintage white Jansz in tastings all round the country every year and people love it. Well, they're going to love this new rosé even more. It's pale salmon pink, with a

lovely, persistent, tiny bubble that lasts for ages in the glass if someone interrupts your drinking by trying to hold a conversation. The flavour foams and swirls round your mouth, creamy yeast mixing with pale strawberry fruit and a delightful fresh texture as soft as beeswax.

nv Champagne Blanc de Blancs, France
Waitrose, £18.99

For years this has been one of the most elegant Champagnes on the market and it's not the first time it's been a winner for us. 'Elegant' is a tricky wine word, overused, often implying lack of oomph. But not here. This has the elegance of a BBC costume drama, of *Pride and Prejudice*, silks and crinolines and parasols. Creamy, soft, caressing your palate, wooing your senses, dismantling the barriers around your soul and teasing you to say 'why not?'

1998 The Black Queen Sparkling Shiraz, Peter Lehmann, South Australia, 14% ABV
Vin du Van, £13.95

This is one of those wines that makes me feel like the bulldog on the Churchill Insurance adverts. 'Oh yes,' I growl, give me some of that. Tasting sparkling wines can be hard work (oh yes it can) – all those bubbles and that acidity make your tonsils sore. And then you pour out this exuberant purple brew. Yes, purple. This is a great big unashamed wodge of ripe black Shiraz that has had the effrontery to add bubbles. It's a big, butch, rich blackcurrant, damson and liquorice Aussie Shiraz dressed up in a pink frothy tutu, legless with mirth. If you've not tried this uproarious happy juice, well, don't blame me, I'm telling you.

2004 Bloomsbury Cuvée Merret, Ridgeview, West Sussex, England, 12% ABV
Waitrose, Butlers Wine Cellar and other independents, £18–£19

The potential for English fizz is massive, and the producers have had a couple of stellar years, winning awards and accolades worldwide. But I feel they're slightly stretched at the moment, perhaps because, for the first time, demand has exceeded supply. Even so, this cuvée from Ridgeview is looking good – quite high in acidity, but that's not unusual with English wines and it means they age extremely well. The fruit is good strong baked apple peel – Bramleys, I should say – and there's honey and yeast there in support. Serious, lean, but good.

2002 Vintage Champagne Brut, Oudinot, France, 12% ABV
Marks & Spencer, £21.99

When I saw the vintage, I thought, that's too young, especially in a serious vintage year like 2002. But the ripeness levels were very high in 2002 and the acid levels were rather low, so it has been possible to release a rich, yeasty, nutty wine, full of youthful foam and bright apple fruit, but mercifully low in acidity. And at five years old, it's ready.

nv Bluff Hill Brut, New Zealand, 12% ABV
Marks & Spencer, £7.99

Loads of class from New Zealand for a bargain price. You'll always get intense fruit in New Zealand fizz – and Chardonnay, Sauvignon and most other things Kiwi – so they've got to keep the fruit in check as well as celebrate it. Which is exactly what they do here. There's loads of rich yeast, a nutty savoury fullness like flaked toasted nuts in muesli, but also good acid fruit and invigorating foam.

nv Champagne Brut Classic, Deutz, France, 12% ABV
Berkmann and independent retailers, £23.99

This was the best of the big-name Champagnes I tried – it's not a mega-name but it's always good. This is classy stuff as usual, though it no longer has a kind of cedar scent that used to mark it out a few years ago. I'd age it another couple of years, but right now it does possess a full soft foam, crunchy fresh apple fruit and a hint of cream that will spread out in time.

Champagne Brut, Mis en Cave 2001, Charles Heidsieck, France, 12% ABV
Booths, £26.99

Just as good as the Deutz (above). If only the other big companies took as much care of their product as Charles Heidsieck does. Year in, year out, this is soft yet lively, dry yet creamy, its acidity charmingly matched by the softness of brioche and the scent of hazelnuts.

nv Champagne, The Wine Society's Private Cuvée Brut (Alfred Gratien), France, 12% ABV
Wine Society, £21

This is not a dainty, retiring flower. There's something of the big beast about it, with fairly rich loft apples baked in muscovado sugar then sprinkled with yeast and tossed about with acidity and foam. It's not a mainstream flavour, but it's good and, if winter's savage this year, it'll be just the stuff to brighten your spirits and keep you warm at the same time.

nv Champagne Brut, Fleury, France, 12.5% ABV
Waitrose, £24.99

A biodynamic wine. I won't go into all the details here, but that means the vineyards are cultivated as naturally as possible, usually in a fairly obsessive way. Which should make for super quality fruit. Well, it's certainly intense – deep loft apple and apple purée flavours, along with some apple and lemon peel acidity and a pretty rich palate. It's a mood fizz; don't choose it if you're feeling frivolous or hysterical.

nv Champagne Oudinot Cuvée Brut, France, 12% ABV
Marks & Spencer, £18.99

M&S are putting some good stuff under their Oudinot label at the moment. This is made mostly from Chardonnay and, although it's fairly young, has a lovely, gentle, soft quality, mild apple fruit rubbing shoulders with hazelnuts wrapped in a mellow coating of cream.

nv Champagne Oudinot Rosé, France, 12% ABV
Marks & Spencer, £21.99

Another good glass from Oudinot, cleverly blending softness with a bit of bite. The fruit is all mild apple flesh, maybe a little squashy strawberry too, and the texture's glycerine soft; but there's a really intriguing twist of black pepper in there which gives it real character. The French sometimes drink Champagne with strawberries and a sprinkling of freshly ground black pepper. I can see it might work.

nv Champagne, Premier Cru Brut (Union Champagne), France, 12% ABV
Tesco, £14.99

Tesco sell so much of this that, despite their best efforts, you can't be quite sure that you'll get it at its absolute best. Even so, it's never worse than good, and is an impressive effort by the producers, a large co-operative group in the best Chardonnay-growing area of Champagne. This is a little leaner than sometimes – it'll probably be creamier by Christmas – but there's good young apple there, attractive acidity and a mellow yeasty cream that will soften the wine over the next few months.

nv Sparkling Shiraz, Banrock Station, South Eastern Australia, 14% ABV
Widely available, £8.49

This is my standby pick-me-up. You can get it all over the place for not much money. It's bursting with easygoing, syrupy plum and blackberry fruit and it makes you giggle and groan as you spill the purple foam all down your shirt. It won't come out, but what the hell.

nv Cabernet Rosé Brut, Ackerman, Loire Valley, France, 12% ABV
Waitrose, £6.99

This is a nice pink fizz, particularly because you can really taste the Cabernet grapes through the bubbles. There's a delightful mild blackcurrant leaf and

raspberry flavour chilled down with chalk from the riverbed, and the foam seems to aid rather than hinder the pleasure.

2006 Prosecco, Vigna Del Cuc, Case Bianche, Martino Zanetti, Veneto, Italy, 11.5% ABV
Bat & Bottle, £8.90

I can see why the Venetians drink so much of this – and I'm not sure why we don't drink more. This is utterly beguiling, with soft pear and apple flesh coated in cream, a hint of floral scent – and it's not quite dry. If it were, it wouldn't be so good.

nv Prosecco, Vincenzo Toffoli, Veneto, Italy, 11.5% ABV
Savage Selection, £7.50

Surprisingly mature for a Prosecco – but that's probably how Mark Savage likes it, and he always follows his own palate in the wines he imports, with some quirky but brilliant results. I can see Mark's point – it's aged very well, keeping its foam and developing a delightful soothing range of flavours: nuts, yeast, a twist of spice and a lick of toffee.

nv Cava Brut, Pinot Noir, Codorníu, Cataluña, Spain, 12% ABV
Majestic, £8.99

Pretty good stuff for a high-volume brand. This is 100 per cent Pinot Noir, and the result is a full, soft wine whose fruit wobbles between strawberry and pink apple. With some yeasty cream and nice refreshing foam, this is very attractive, widely available pink fizz.

nv Cava Reserva Brut Rosado, Palau Gazo, Spain, 11.5% ABV
Booths, £5.49

Good blushing bubbly. It's pretty dry, has a lovely caressing foam and a really interesting flavour of ripe apple, some red plum flesh and a touch of rosehip scent.

2005 Vintage Cava Brut (Codorníu), Cataluña, Spain, 11.5% ABV
Sainsbury's Taste the Difference, £9.99

Classy fizz made by the giant Codorníu, mostly from Chardonnay, so you get ripe apple fruit, soft and fresh, good yeasty cream but also an unexpected and attractive hint of green peppercorns to tone up your palate.

nv Cava Brut, Vineyard X (Covides), Cataluña, Spain, 11.5% ABV
Threshers, £4.99 (3 for 2, £3.33)

This has to be the party fizz for this Christmas – it's fresh, spicy and really quite mellow. Add a cool label and the party's already humming.

SWEETIES

Look, it's not that I don't like sweet wines. I do. At their best they're sex on wheels. But I taste less and less of them. And I fear you are tasting less and less of them too. Wine styles go in and out of fashion. Sweet wines had their salad days at the end of the 1990s. This century, well, they've teetered – though some smashing stuff is being made – but to be honest, most high street retailers don't even bother to show their sweet wines at tastings any more. We don't see 'em. We don't write about 'em. You don't drink 'em. Even so, here's a small but merry band of goodies.

2005 Eiswein, Welschriesling, Hölzler, Weinrieder, Austria, 10.5% ABV
Waterloo Wine Company, £15/375ml

Now this is a beauty. Austria has an array of wine producers who excel at gooey, sticky delights like this, and their genius lies in managing to preserve an invigorating acidity and a taut streak of minerality while the richness of succulent fruit threatens to swamp your senses. Here, the flavours assault your palate in waves, at first a viscous flood of peach syrup, custard cream and ripe apricot skins, but this is rapidly followed by the zing of citrus orange acidity and a growing minerality halfway between the stony dryness of rock dust and the childhood memory of putty on a window frame.

2002 Botrytis Riesling-Gewurztraminer, La Magia, Joseph, Primo Estate, South Australia, 10.5% ABV
Philglas & Swiggot, £11.50/375ml

The great aromatic German grapes magicked into a thrilling nectar by an Italian immigrant in the hothouse of Australia. Well, that's the true Australia for you – no rules or stuffy traditions, just find out what works and do it as best you can. Joe Grilli set out to amaze the wine world with his talents in some very unpromising furnace-hot flatlands north of Adelaide. He's now managed to move to the more quality-conscious environs of McLaren Vale, just south of Adelaide, and is sourcing some fantastic fruit. This is memorable stuff, full of fascinating, unexpected twists and turns of flavour – part as fat and baked as marmalade, part as luscious as pineapple drenched in syrup, and part as fresh as strawberries, as green herbs, as springtime orchard apple blossom.

2005 Botrytis Riesling, Tamar Ridge, Tasmania, Australia, 9% ABV
deFINE, Great Western Wine, Lay & Wheeler and other independent retailers, £13.95/375ml

Tasmania isn't well known for sweet wines and the guys at Tamar Ridge admit they hardly ever get the right conditions. To make this one, they had to leave the grapes on the vines until June – in northern hemisphere terms, that's the run-up to Christmas. But it's worth it for this beautifully delicate Riesling. The acidity of green apple and lemon peel occasionally surges with an intensity nearer that of cider vinegar, but then it eases back and lets a delightful fresh heather-scented honey take over again.

2004 Botrytis Semillon, Hermits Hill (De Bortoli), Riverina, New South Wales, Australia, 11.5% ABV
Marks & Spencer, £5.99/375ml

This wine is made out in bandit country, miles from anywhere – well, the place is called Griffith but, believe me, it is miles from anywhere. Even so, one thing that occurs every year is a whopping great infection of 'noble rot' to sweeten the grapes. This isn't the sweetest wine they make up there – but look at the price. It's expensive to make sweet wine. £5.99 is a bargain for this deep, rich wine packed with pineapple and toffee cream and rippled with barbecue smoke.

2004 Botrytis Semillon, Keith Tulloch, Hunter Valley, New South Wales, Australia, 14% ABV
Vin du Van, £11.95/375ml

To make a naturally sweet wine you generally need to use grapes infected by a delightful phenomenon called 'noble rot' – a rare benign fungus that intensifies the grapes' sweetness rather than turning them to vinegar. It doesn't occur very often in Australia's Hunter Valley, just north of Sydney. Rot occurs a lot, since they frequently get torrential storms just before harvest – but it isn't noble. Somehow Keith Tulloch managed to fill his pail full of nicely rotten grapes and he's made a rich marmaladey wine, already mature and packed with sweet peach fruit speckled with ginger spice.

2004 Monbazillac, Domaine du Haut-Rauly, South-West France, 13% ABV
Co-op, £4.79/375ml

What makes this so enjoyable is a texture as lush and languid as beeswax. There's wax in the flavour too, rather like freshly waxed leather, to keep a savoury suggestion in a wine that is otherwise thick with pineapple and peach and sweet lazy syrup. This will age into the classic Sauternes flavours of pineapple and barley sugar, but it's sumptuous now, so why wait?

Rutherglen Muscat, Campbells, Victoria, Australia, 17.5% ABV
Oddbins, £8.49/375ml

You could argue that this is a fortified wine. Actually, when they fortify Liqueur Muscat the liquid hasn't usually begun to ferment properly, so if you're in an argumentative mood you could say it's not really a wine at all. But you can't argue about its sweetness, the lush, heady, hothouse-scented sweetness of Muscat grapes dripping with syrupy juice, coating your tongue with exotic honeyed goo, making your head spin with the sheer indulgence of it all. So I reckon it fits into the sweeties section pretty neatly.

1971 Don PX Gran Reserva, Montilla-Moriles, Andalusia, Spain, 17% ABV
Butlers Wine Cellar, les Caves de Pyrene, Moreno Wines,
£11.99–12.99/375ml

This wine is so thick and unctuous that when you swirl it in the glass, a day later the syrupy liquid is still oozing back down the sides at glacial speed, leaving a black treacle trail behind. Empty the glass. Leave it another day, and the aroma, far from evaporating, has intensified into a palate-blasting pottage of everything rich and brown. It is *intensely* sweet, with the sort of sweetness that hurts your teeth when you're chewing raisins or sultanas. But it also has a lively acidity and a savoury depth of beef stew, burnt and smoky from simmering too long in the pan. And one more thing: this is 37 years old, and it only costs just over a tenner.

FORTIFIED WINES

Just as I was about to continue my moan of last year that the standard of own-label and supermarket sherries and ports was on the slide and that they were being inexplicably and pointlessly dumbed down, I thought I'd better have one last look at what's available on the high street. And a smile comes back to my face. Quality is on the up again. In particular the sherries are beginning to bristle with more self-confident flavours. This is absolutely crucial. The sherry producers tried the cheap and not-so-cheerful route a generation ago: it bankrupted half the producing companies and alienated exactly the enthusiastic wine drinkers they should have been trying to woo.

• This section begins with tangy, appetizing sherries – best served ice-cold – and ends with some rich and warming ports.

Manzanilla Extra Dry Sherry, Marks & Spencer (Williams & Humbert), Spain, 15% ABV
Marks & Spencer, £4.99

M&S are making a bit of a speciality out of their Manzanilla sherry, and we seem to be buying it. That's great news because, with Manzanilla, freshness is everything; it needs to be bottled regularly throughout the year, rushed to England and rapidly consumed by us. I don't pretend that Manzanilla sherry is a mainstream flavour. No true sherry is a mainstream flavour – sweetened, softened Pale Cream is 'mainstream', and that's light years away from the true taste of Andalusia. Sourness, pungency and austerity are the key, surprising, shocking flavours that rattle on your palate's door and brace your appetite and make dry sherry such an effective aperitif. This challenging marriage of loft apples and old wooden floors, sourdough bread yeast and the affectionate rub of cold dry leather achieves all that triumphantly.

Manzanilla Pale Dry Sherry, Sainsbury's (Emilio Lustau), Spain, 15% ABV
Sainsbury's, £4.99

Most sherry is blended in big barrels from various sources. But Sainsbury's get their Manzanilla from one guy in Spain who hoards his barrels unblended with anyone else's. And the result is that you definitely get the bread yeast and loft apple flavours, tart yet mouthfilling, you get the dusty dryness of banisters at the top of a rickety old staircase, but you also get an extra savoury element like a whiff of grilled meat or a dab of fish paste (hey, I loved fish paste when I was a kid) that makes it stand out appetizingly from the crowd.

Tanners Mariscal Manzanilla, Dolores Bustillo Delgado, Spain, 15% ABV
Tanners, £6.80

I really need to see a photo of Dolores Bustillo Delgado. Until then, her wine must do – gentle, not as salt-savoury as some Manzanillas, but still with the rasp of dry old wood, although the suggestion of buttered brazils almost makes me think she tripped up by the barrel and tipped a jug of Amontillado in by mistake.

La Copita Fino, Spain, 15% ABV
Oddbins, £6.99

Fino sherries are created a little further inland than Manzanillas and don't get the same sea breeze to cool their brow and fleck it with salt as they age. The result is a slightly fuller, broader wine but one that is still defined by the rich, sour flavours of bread yeast and old loft apples, the crunchy paleness of nut flesh and the stone dry mist of summer dust.

Dry Amontillado Sherry, aged 12 years, (Emilio Lustau), Spain, 19% ABV
Sainsbury's Taste the Difference, £6.99/50 cl

Dry Amontillado is an endangered species. Too many vicars and spinster aunts have been served up sweetish brownish pap under the name Amontillado and its reputation has dived. But real Amontillado is bone dry yet amazingly rich, with a nutty flavour no other wine can match. This is excellent stuff, with that strangely attractive sweet paper smell of a Manila envelope bulging with buttered brazils and dry dates, and that's the flavour too – concentrated, satisfying, with a pungent sour streak that is refreshing and delightful.

East India Solera, Emilio Lustau, Spain, 20% ABV
Sainsbury's, Waitrose and independent retailers, £7.99/50 cl

East India Solera – what a beautifully evocative name, speaking of another era, other customs, other flavours. Well, this is almost out of time and place – a lovely sweet sherry of real quality rather than the stewy sugar-water most cheap sherry is. This has all the richness of dates and sultanas at their sweetest, balanced by sweet-sour acidity, everything enveloped in an old, old shade of brown.

Zuleta Amontillado Viejo, Delgado Zuleta, Spain, 19.5% ABV
Tanners, £17.40

This is as challenging as a mouthful of sherry gets. Viejo means old, and by God this reeks of oldness – old banisters, old parquet, old aunts, old ribs of beef. But the great joy of Amontillado is its dry yet lush richness of buttered brazils – creamy nut encased in crackly caramel – and here it is, sweeping up the cobwebs and the frock coats as it goes. But I warn you, this is extreme sherry.

Solera 1847 Sweet Cream Sherry, González Byass, Spain, 18% ABV
Waitrose, £9.55

Gentle but deep, rich wine, properly sweet from good grapes and old wine, not just casually sugared up. Big, soft dates, figs and sultana toffee-rich fruit tempered by balsamic vinegar acidity.

Rich Cream Sherry, Marks & Spencer (Williams & Humbert), Spain, 17% ABV
Marks & Spencer, £5.99

Maybe it says something about their customer base, but M&S always seem to have a good cream sherry. Perhaps they just say 'don't change a thing' on each buying visit. Well, since the heart of a good sweet sherry lies in blending well-aged components together, this is probably the best possible request to make – and I suspect people who like sweet sherry aren't too keen on change in any case. This has real syrupy power – figs and dates and glycerine all sloshing about with buttered brazils and a cleansing balsamic vinegar streak of acidity. M&S also do a 'Sweet Cream Sherry'. This 'Rich' one is the same price, and better.

1995 Vintage Port, Quinta da Roeda, Croft, Portugal, 20.5% ABV
Majestic, £15.99

When the label says 'Vintage Port' my expectations are high – and so they should be. A vintage port, from a single harvest, as against most port which is a blend of harvests, should be the quality pinnacle for a producer, since only a tiny amount of their annual crop will be released as Vintage. But usually the price is way over £20, so I was wary when I saw this on Majestic's shelves for £15.99. I needn't have been. It's a cracker. Relatively mature at 12 years old, it's sublimely balanced and, although you are aware of a little black pepper spice and a flicker of fiery spirit deep in the heart of the wine, the flavour is dark and lush and intense – blackcurrants, blackberries, damsons and morello cherries all squeezed together in the superripe richness and lovin' it.

1998 Vintage Port, Taylor's Quinta de Vargellas, Portugal, 20.5% ABV
Majestic, Oddbins, Sainsbury's, Tesco, £24.99

Dark, powerful, serious stuff. In an ideal world I'd age this for a good few years yet, because it is a rough, rich, coarse-chopped kind of style with vegetable savoury flavours and tannin gobbled up by black sweet fruit. But if you're in the mood …

2000 Vintage Port, Quinta do Crasto, Portugal, 20% ABV
Sainsbury's Taste the Difference, £19.99

This is big, baked stuff, stuffed with a thicket of rich stewed loganberry and damson fruit. It's rich, sweet and powerful and, if you drink it now, make sure you're sitting down and don't have early appointments the next day. Of course, you could age it – it'll soften and gain scent over five to ten years – and I think I'd buy two: one for this year and one for under the stairs and who knows when I'll get the urge.

Tanners Crusted Port, bottled 2001 (Churchill Graham), Portugal, 19.5% ABV
Tanners, £13.95

Crusted is a fabulous semi-vintage kind of port – vintage port in short trousers – a British curiosity that we have fought to save from the EU who wanted to ban it. Why? Probably because it tasted good, didn't cost the earth and the Brits lapped it up. Well, savour it while you can: this is dense, powerful, solid stuff full of pepper attack and a swipe of spirity fire, but that's easily overwhelmed by a welter of blackberry, black plum and loganberry fruit all swathed in the richness of toffee.

Reserve Port, Terra Prima, Fonseca (organically grown grapes), Portugal, 20% ABV
Sainsbury's, £10.99

Ideally, I'd age this wine – and I'm sure it would happily age 10 years – because it is very young. But it's also very good and isn't too brash or mighty to provide youthful fun. In fact, though it's quite a big beast it

isn't a hairy beast, unkempt, aggressive. It actually has perfume – somewhere between the scent of violets and the mild aroma of rosehip – it has creamy texture and fruit which is rich and dark red rather than brutal black.

2001 The Society's LBV Port (Symington Family Estates), Portugal, 20% ABV
The Wine Society, £9.95

The quality of LBV (late bottled vintage) ports in the high street is a bit patchy at the moment, but, typically, The Wine Society has sourced some good stuff from one of the biggest producers. This is made in the modern, non-artisan way and is forced through a filter to avoid sediment forming (traditional ports don't go near a filter machine). The result is nonetheless impressive: powerful, not beautiful, the texture dense rather than delicate, but when my palate is blockaded by such a wodge of blackberry and sweet plum with a swathe of black pepper fire playing pinball on my tongue – I'll take it.

The Society's Exhibition 10 Year Old Tawny Port, Portugal, 20% ABV
The Wine Society, £14.95

In a way, the exact opposite of the vintage port style (see page 133) but absolutely delightful in its own manner. There's less fire in the belly, more delicacy and charm and calm repose in the glance. The colour isn't bold, but is a mellow tawny blushed with pink. The pink shows that a little of the youthful blackberry fruit and herb scent still lingers, but the wine is now full of brown beauty, autumnal, reflective, quince and medlar, sultana and date and the dry wood aroma of an Edwardian drawing room.

10-year-old Tawny Port, Taylor's, Portugal, 20% ABV
Booths, Majestic, Sainsbury's, Selfridges, Tesco, Threshers, £16.99

A very attractive tawny port which I think I'd serve fairly cool. It's relatively light, but that's fine for a tawny – brawny tawny I don't want. There's also just a lick of tannic roughness as though someone had thrown a few sticks of liquorice into the barrel. But the overall effect is mellow – a whiff of cigar smoke, a mild richness of date and sultana which dallies with your palate, and a fragile memory of fading youth shown by a touch of plum sweetness and spice.

10-year-old Tawny Port, Warres Otima, Portugal, 20% ABV
Oddbins, £10.99/50 cl

This smells a bit adolescent and frisky, and does have a pink caste to its tawny brown, but it's a very attractive rich mix of raisin and date and nut flesh steeped in the ripe red flesh of recent youth.

Storing, serving and tasting

Wine is all about enjoyment, so don't let anyone make you anxious about opening, serving, tasting and storing it. Here are some tips to help you enjoy your wine all the more.

The corkscrew

The first step in tasting any wine is to extract the cork. Look for a corkscrew with an open spiral and a comfortable handle. The Screwpull brand is far and away the best, with a high-quality open spiral. 'Waiter's friend' corkscrews – the type you see used in restaurants – are good too, once you get the knack.

Corkscrews with a solid core that looks like a giant woodscrew tend to mash up delicate corks or get stuck in tough ones. And try to avoid those 'butterfly' corkscrews with the twin lever arms and a bottle opener on the end; they tend to leave cork crumbs floating in the wine.

Corks

Don't be a cork snob. The only requirements for the seal on a bottle of wine are that it should be hygienic, airtight, long-lasting and removable. Real cork is environmentally friendly, but is prone to shrinkage and infection, which can taint the wine. Synthetic closures modelled on the traditional cork are common in budget wines and are increasingly used by high-quality producers, as are screwcaps, or Stelvin closures.

Decanting

Transferring wine to a decanter brings it into contact with oxygen, which can open up the flavours. You don't need to do it ages before serving and you don't need a special decanter: a glass jug is just as good. And there's no reason why you shouldn't decant the wine to aerate it, then pour it back into its bottle to serve it.

Mature red wine is likely to contain sediment and needs careful handling. Stand the bottle upright for a day or two to let the sediment fall to the bottom. Open the wine carefully, and place a torch or candle beside the decanter. As you pour, stand so that you can see the light shining through the neck of the bottle. Pour the wine into the decanter in one steady motion and stop when you see the sediment reaching the neck of the bottle.

Temperature

The temperature of wine has a bearing on its flavour. Heavy reds are happy at room temperature, but the lighter the wine the cooler it should be. I'd serve Burgundy and other Pinot Noir reds at cool larder temperature. Juicy, fruity young reds, such as wines from the Loire Valley, are refreshing served lightly chilled.

Chilling white wines makes them taste fresher, but also subdues flavours, so bear this in mind if you're splashing out on a top-quality white – don't keep it in the fridge too long. Sparkling wines, however, must be well chilled to avoid exploding corks and fountains of foam.

For quick chilling, fill a bucket with ice and cold water, plus a few spoonfuls of salt if you're in a real hurry. This is much more effective than ice on its own. If the wine is already cool a vacuum-walled cooler will maintain the temperature.

The wine glass

The ideal wine glass is a fairly large tulip shape, made of fine, clear glass, with a slender stem. This shape helps to concentrate the aromas of the wine and to show off its colours and texture. For sparkling wine choose a tall, slender glass, as it helps the bubbles to last longer.

Look after your glasses carefully. Detergent residues or grease can affect the flavour of any wine and reduce the bubbliness of sparkling wine. Ideally, wash glasses in very hot water and don't use detergent at all. Rinse glasses thoroughly and allow them to air-dry. Store wine glasses upright to avoid trapping stale odours.

Keeping opened bottles

Exposure to oxygen causes wine to deteriorate. It lasts fairly well if you just push the cork back in and stick the bottle in the fridge, but you can also buy a range of effective devices to help keep oxygen at bay. Vacuvin uses a rubber stopper and a vacuum pump to remove air from the bottle. Others inject inert gas into the bottle to shield the wine from the ravages of oxidation.

Laying down wine

The longer you intend to keep wine, the more important it is to store it with care. If you haven't got a cellar, find a nook – under the stairs, a built-in cupboard or a disused fireplace – that is cool, relatively dark and vibration-free, in which you can store the bottles on their sides to keep the corks moist (if a cork dries out it will let air in and spoil the wine).

Wine should be kept cool – around 10–15°C/50–55°F. It is also important to avoid sudden temperature changes or extremes: a windowless garage or outhouse may be cool in summer but may freeze in winter. Exposure to light can ruin wine, but dark bottles go some way to protecting it from light.

How to taste wine

If you just knock your wine back like a cold beer, you'll be missing most of whatever flavour it has to offer. Take a bit of time to pay attention to what you're tasting and I guarantee you'll enjoy the wine more.

Read the label

There's no law that says you have to make life hard for yourself when tasting wine. So have a look at what you're drinking and read the notes on the back label if there is one. The label will tell you the vintage, the region and/or the grape variety, the producer and the alcohol level.

Look at the wine

Pour the wine into a glass so it is a third full and tilt it against a white background so you can enjoy the range of colours in the wine. Is it dark or light? Is it viscous or watery? As you gain experience the look of the wine will tell you one or two things about the age and the likely flavour and weight of the wine. As a wine ages, whites lose their springtime greenness and gather deeper, golden hues, whereas red wines trade the purple of youth for a paler brick red.

Swirl and sniff

Give the glass a vigorous swirl to wake up the aromas in the wine, stick your nose in and inhale gently. This is where you'll be hit by the amazing range of smells a wine can produce. Interpret them in any way that means something to you personally: it's only by reacting honestly to the taste and smell of a wine that you can build up a memory bank of flavours against which to judge future wines.

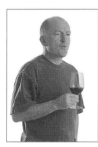

Take a sip

At last! It's time to drink the wine. So take a decent-sized slurp – enough to fill your mouth about a third full. The tongue can detect only very basic flavour elements: sweetness at the tip, acidity at the sides and bitterness at the back. The real business of tasting goes on in a cavity at the back of the mouth which is really part of the nose. The idea is to get the fumes from the wine to rise up into this nasal cavity. Note the toughness, acidity and sweetness of the wine, then suck some air through the wine to help the flavours on their way. Gently 'chew' the wine and let it coat your tongue, teeth, cheeks and gums. Jot down a few notes as you form your opinion and then make the final decision… Do you like it or don't you?

Swallow or spit it out

If you are tasting a lot of wines, you will have to spit as you go if you want to remain upright and retain your judgement. Otherwise, go ahead and swallow and enjoy the lovely aftertaste of the wine.

Wine Faults

If you order wine in a restaurant and you find one of these faults you are entitled to a replacement. Many retailers will also replace a faulty bottle if you return it the day after you open it, with your receipt. Sometimes faults affect random bottles, others may ruin a whole case of wine.

- Cork taint – a horrible musty, mouldy smell indicates 'corked' wine, caused by a contaminated cork
- Volatile acidity – pronounced vinegary or acetone smells
- Oxidation – sherry-like smells are not appropriate in red and white wines
- Hydrogen sulphide – 'rotten eggs' smell.

Watchpoints

- Sediment in red wines makes for a gritty, woody mouthful. To avoid this, either decant the wine or simply pour it gently, leaving the last few centilitres of wine in the bottle.
- White crystals, or tartrates, on the cork or at the bottom of bottles of white wine are both harmless and flavourless.
- Sticky bottle neck – if wine has seeped past the cork it probably hasn't been very well kept and air might have got in. This may mean oxidized wine.
- Excess sulphur dioxide is sometimes noticeable as a smell of a recently struck match; it should dissipate after a few minutes.

Wine style guide

When faced with a shelf – or a screen – packed with wines from around the world, where do you start? Well, if you're after a particular flavour, my guide to wine styles will point you in the right direction.

White Wines

Bone-dry, neutral whites

Neutral wines exist for the sake of seafood or to avoid interrupting you while you're eating. It's a question of balance, rather than aromas and flavours, but there will be a bit of lemon, yeast and a mineral thrill in a good Muscadet sur lie or a proper Chablis. Loads of Italian whites do the same thing, but Italy is increasingly picking up on the global shift towards fruit flavours and maybe some oak. Basic, cheap South African whites are often a good bet if you want something thirst-quenching and easy to drink. Colombard and Chenin are fairly neutral grape varieties widely used in South Africa, often producing appley flavours, and better examples add a lick of honey.

- Muscadet
- Chenin Blanc and Colombard – from the Loire Valley, South-West France, Australia, California or South Africa
- Basic white Bordeaux and Entre-Deux-Mers
- Chablis
- Pinot Grigio

Green, tangy whites

For nerve-tingling refreshment, Sauvignon Blanc is the classic grape, full of fresh grass, gooseberry and nettle flavours. I always used to go for New Zealand versions, but I'm now more inclined to reach for an inexpensive bottle from Chile, South Africa or Hungary. Or even a simple white Bordeaux, because suddenly

Bordeaux Sauvignon is buzzing with life. Most Sancerre and the other Loire Sauvignons are overpriced. Austria's Grüner Veltliner has a peppery freshness. From north-west Iberia, Galicia's Albariño grape has a stony, mineral lemon zest sharpness; the same grape is used in Portugal, for Vinho Verde. Alternatively, look at Riesling: Australia serves it up with aggressive lime and mineral flavours, and New Zealand and Chile give milder versions of the same style. Alsace Riesling is lemony and dry, while German Rieslings go from bone-dry to intensely sweet, with the tangiest, zestiest, coming from the Mosel Valley.

- Sauvignon Blanc – from New Zealand, Chile, Hungary, South Africa, or Bordeaux
- Loire Valley Sauvignons such as Sancerre and Pouilly-Fumé
- Riesling – from Australia, Austria, Chile, Germany, New Zealand, or Alsace in France
- Austrian Grüner Veltliner
- Vinho Verde from Portugal and Albariño from north-west Spain

Intense, nutty whites

The best white Burgundy from the Côte d'Or cannot be bettered for its combination of soft nut and oatmeal flavours, subtle, buttery oak and firm, dry structure. Prices are often hair-raising and the cheaper wines rarely offer much Burgundy style. For £7 or £8 your best bet is oaked Chardonnay from an innovative Spanish region such as Somontano or Navarra. You'll get a nutty, creamy taste and nectarine fruit with good oak-aged white Bordeaux or traditional white Rioja. Top Chardonnays from New World countries – and Italy for that matter – can emulate Burgundy, but once again we're looking at serious prices.

- White Burgundy – including Meursault, Pouilly-Fuissé, Chassagne-Montrachet, Puligny-Montrachet
- White Bordeaux – including Pessac-Léognan, Graves
- White Rioja
- Chardonnay from New Zealand and Oregon – and top examples from Australia, California and South Africa

Ripe, tropical whites

Aussie Chardonnay conquered the world with its upfront flavours of peaches, apricots and melons, usually spiced up by the vanilla, toast and butterscotch richness of new oak. This winning style has now become a standard-issue flavour produced by all sorts of countries, though I still love the original. You'll need to spend a bit more than a fiver nowadays if you want something to relish beyond the first glass. Oaked Australian Semillon can also give rich, ripe fruit flavours, as can oaked Chenin Blanc from New Zealand and South Africa. If you see the words 'unoaked' or 'cool-climate' on an Aussie bottle, expect an altogether leaner drink.

- Chardonnay: from Australia, Chile, California
- Oak-aged Chenin Blanc from New Zealand and South Africa
- Australian Semillon

Aromatic whites

Alsace has always been a plentiful source of perfumed, dry or off-dry whites: Gewurztraminer with its rose and lychee scent or Muscat with its floral, hothouse grape perfume. A few producers in New Zealand, Australia, Chile and South Africa are having some success with these grapes. Floral, apricotty Viognier, traditionally the grape of Condrieu in the northern Rhône, now appears in vins de pays from all over southern France and also from California and Australia. Condrieu is expensive (£20 will get you entry-level stuff and no guarantee that it will be fragrant); vin de pays wines start at around £5 and are just as patchy. For aroma on a budget grab some Hungarian Irsai Olivér or Argentinian Torrontés. English white wines often have a fresh, floral hedgerow scent – the Bacchus grape is one of the leaders of this style.

- Alsace whites, especially Gewurztraminer and Muscat
- Gewürztraminer from Austria, Chile, Germany, New Zealand and cooler regions of Australia
- Condrieu, from the Rhône Valley in France
- Viognier from southern France, Argentina, Australia, California, Chile
- English white wines
- Irsai Olivér from Hungary
- Torrontés from Argentina

Golden, sweet whites

Good sweet wines are difficult to make and therefore expensive: prices for Sauternes and Barsac (from Bordeaux) can go through the roof, but near-neighbours Monbazillac, Loupiac, Saussignac and Ste-Croix-du-Mont are more affordable. Sweet Loire wines such as Quarts de Chaume, Bonnezeaux and some Vouvrays have a quince aroma and a fresh acidity that can keep them lively for decades, as do sweet Rieslings, such as Alsace Vendange Tardive, German and Austrian Beerenauslese (BA), Trockenbeerenauslese (TBA) and Eiswein. Canadian icewine is quite rare over here, but we're seeing more of Hungary's Tokaji, with its sweet-sour, marmalade flavours.

- Sauternes, Barsac, Loupiac, Sainte-Croix-du-Mont
- Monbazillac, Saussignac
- Loire sweet whites such as Bonnezeaux, Quarts de Chaume and Vouvray moelleux
- Auslese, Beerenauslese and Trockenbeerenauslese from Germany and Austria
- Eiswein from Germany, icewine from Canada
- Botrytis Semillon, Riesling or Gewürztraminer from Australia

Red wines
Juicy, fruity reds

The definitive modern style for easygoing reds. Tasty, refreshing and delicious with or without food, they pack in loads of crunchy fruit while minimizing the tough, gum-drying tannins that characterize most traditional red wine styles. Beaujolais (made from the Gamay grape) is the prototype: the excellent 2005 vintage delivered juicy fruit by the bucketful, and 2006 was pretty good too – you're likely to find both vintages in the shops now. And if you're distinctly underwhelmed by the very mention of the word 'Beaujolais', remember that the delightfully named Fleurie, St-Amour and Chiroubles also come from the Beaujolais region. Loire reds such as Chinon and Saumur (made from Cabernet Franc) pack in the fresh raspberries. Italy's Bardolino is light and refreshing, as is young Valpolicella. Nowadays, hi-tech producers all over the world are working the magic with a whole host of grape varieties. Carmenère, Malbec and Merlot are always good bets, and Grenache/Garnacha and Tempranillo usually come up with the goods. Italian grapes like Bonarda, Barbera and Sangiovese seem to double in succulence under Argentina's blazing sun. And at around £5 even Cabernet Sauvignon – if it's from somewhere warm like Australia, South America, South Africa or Spain – or a vin de pays Syrah from southern France, will emphasize the fruit and hold back on the tannin.

- Beaujolais – including Brouilly, Chiroubles, Fleurie, Juliénas, Moulin-à-Vent, St-Amour. Also wines made from the Gamay grape in other parts of France
- Loire reds: Chinon, Saumur, Saumur-Champigny – and, if you're lucky, Bourgueil, Cheverny and St-Nicolas de Bourgueil
- Grenache (from France) and Garnacha (from Spain)
- Carmenère from Chile and basic Merlot from just about anywhere
- Inexpensive Argentinian reds, especially Bonarda, but also Sangiovese and Tempranillo

Silky, strawberryish reds

Here we're looking for some special qualities, specifically a gorgeously smooth texture and a heavenly fragrance of strawberries, raspberries or cherries. We're looking for soft, decadent, seductive wines. One grape – Pinot Noir – and one region – Burgundy – stand out, but prices are high to astronomical. Good red Burgundy is addictively hedonistic and all sorts of strange decaying aromas start to hover around the strawberries as the wine ages. Pinot Noirs from New Zealand, California, Oregon and, increasingly, Australia come close, but they're expensive, too; Chilean Pinots are far more affordable. You can get that strawberry perfume (though not the silky texture) from other grapes in Spain's Navarra, Rioja and up-coming regions like La Mancha and Murcia. Southern Rhône blends can deliver if you look for fairly light examples of Côtes du Rhône-Villages or Costières de Nîmes.

- Red Burgundy – including Chassagne-Montrachet, Beaune, Givry, Nuits-St-Georges, Pommard
- Pinot Noir from Australia, California, Chile, New Zealand, Oregon
- Spanish reds from Rioja, Navarra, La Mancha and Valdepeñas, especially with Tempranillo as the main grape
- Red blends from the southern Rhône Valley, such as Costières de Nîmes, Côtes du Rhône-Villages, Gigondas
- Australian Grenache

Intense, blackcurrancy reds

Firm, intense wines which often only reveal their softer side with a bit of age; Cabernet Sauvignon is the grape, on its own or blended with Merlot or other varieties. Bordeaux is the classic region but there are far too many overpriced underachievers there. And Cabernet's image has changed. You can still choose the austere, tannic style, in theory aging to a heavenly cassis and cedar maturity, but most of the world is taking a fruitier blackcurrant-and-mint approach. Chile does the fruity style par excellence. New Zealand can deliver Bordeaux-like flavours, but in a faster-maturing wine. Australia often adds a medicinal eucalyptus twist or a dollop of blackcurrant jam. Argentina and South Africa are making their mark too.

- Bordeaux reds such as Côtes de Castillon, St-Émilion, Pomerol
- Cabernet Sauvignon from just about anywhere
- Cabernet Sauvignon-Merlot blends

Spicy, warm-hearted reds

Australian Shiraz is the epitome of this rumbustious, riproaring style: dense, rich, chocolaty, sometimes with a twist of pepper, a whiff of smoke, or a slap of leather. But it's not alone. There are southern Italy's Primitivo and Nero d'Avola, California's Zinfandel, Mexico's Petite Sirah, Argentina's Malbec, South Africa's Pinotage, Toro from Spain and some magnificent Greek reds. In southern France the wines of the Languedoc often show this kind of warmth, roughed up with hillside herbs. And if you want your spice more serious, more smoky and minerally, go for the classic wines of the northern Rhône Valley.

- Australian Shiraz, as well blends of Shiraz with Grenache and Mourvèdre/Mataro – and Durif
- Northern Rhône Syrah (Cornas, Côte-Rôtie, Hermitage, St-Joseph) and southern Rhône blends such as Châteauneuf-du-Pape
- Southern French reds, such as Corbières, Coteaux du Languedoc, Côtes du Roussillon, Faugères, Fitou, Minervois
- Italian reds such as Primitivo, Aglianico, Negroamaro and Nero d'Avola
- Zinfandel and Petite Sirah reds
- Argentinian Malbec

Mouthwatering, sweet-sour reds

Sounds weird? This style is primarily the preserve of Italy, and it's all about food: the rasp of sourness cuts through rich, meaty food, with a lip-smacking tingle that works equally well with pizza or tomato-based pasta dishes. But there's fruit in there too – cherries and plums – plus raisiny sweetness and a herby bite. The wines are now better made than ever, with more seductive fruit, but holding on to those fascinating flavours. All sorts of native Italian grape varieties deliver this delicious sour-cherries taste: Sangiovese (the classic red grape of Tuscany), Nebbiolo (from Piedmont), Barbera. Dolcetto, Teroldego, Sagrantino… You'll have to shell out up to a tenner for decent Chianti, more for Piedmont wines (especially Barolo and Barbaresco, so try Langhe instead). Valpolicella can be very good, but choose with care. Portugal reveals something of the same character in its reds.

- Chianti, plus other wines made from the Sangiovese grape
- Barolo, Barbaresco and other wines made from the Nebbiolo grape
- Valpolicella Classico, Amarone della Valpolicella
- Southern Italian reds
- Touriga Nacional and other Portuguese reds

Delicate (and not-so-delicate) Rosé

Dry rosé can be wonderful, with flavours of strawberries and maybe raspberries and rosehips, cherries, apples and herbs, too. Look for wines made from sturdy grapes like Cabernet, Syrah or Merlot, or go for Grenache/Garnacha or Tempranillo from Spain and the Rhône Valley. South America is a good bet for flavoursome, fruit-forward pink wine. *See pages 102–7 for my top pinks this year.*

Drink organic – or even biodynamic

- The widely discussed benefits of organic farming – respect for the environment, minimal chemical residues in our food and drink – apply to grapes as much as to any other produce. Full-blown organic viticulture forbids the use of synthetic fertilizers, herbicides or fungicides; instead, cover crops and companion planting encourage biodiversity and natural predators to keep the soil and vines healthy. Warm, dry climates like the South of France, Chile and South Africa have the advantage of rarely suffering from the damp that can cause rot, mildew and other problems – we should be seeing more organic wines from these regions. Organic wines from European countries are often labelled 'Biologique', or simply 'Bio'.
- Biodynamic viticulture takes working with nature one stage further: work in the vineyard is planned in accordance with the movements of the planets, moon, sun and cosmic forces to achieve health and balance in the soil and in the vine. Vines are treated with infusions of mineral, animal and plant materials, applied in homeopathic quantities, with some astonishing results.
- If you want to know more, the best companies to contact are Vinceremos and Vintage Roots.

Sparkling Wines

Champagne can be the finest sparkling wine on the planet, but fizz made by the traditional Champagne method in Australia, New Zealand or California – often using the same grape varieties – is often just as good and cheaper. It might be a little more fruity, where Champagne concentrates on bready, yeasty or nutty aromas, but a few are dead ringers for the classic style. Fizz is also made in other parts of France: Crémant de Bourgogne is one of the best. England is beginning to show its potential. Italy's Prosecco is soft and delicately scented. Spain's Cava is perfect party fizz available at bargain basement prices in all the big supermarkets.

• Champagne
• Traditional method fizz made from Chardonnay, Pinot Noir and Pinot Meunier grapes grown in Australia, California, England, New Zealand, South Africa
• Cremant de Bourgogne, Cremant de Loire, Cremant de Jura, Cremant d'Alsace, Blanquette de Limoux
• Cava
• Prosecco
• Sparkling Shiraz – an Aussie speciality – will make a splash at a wild party

Fortified Wines

Tangy, appetizing fortified wines

To set your taste buds tingling, fino and manzanilla sherries are pale, perfumed, bone dry and bracingly tangy. True amontillado, dark and nutty, is also dry. Dry oloroso adds deep, raisiny flavours. Palo cortado falls between amontillado and oloroso; manzanilla pasada is an older, nuttier manzanilla. The driest style of Madeira, Sercial, is steely and smoky; Verdelho Madeira is a bit fuller and richer, but still tangy and dry.

• Manzanilla and fino sherry
• Dry Amontillado, palo cortado and dry oloroso sherry
• Sercial and Verdelho Madeira

Rich, warming fortified wines

Raisins and brown sugar, dried figs and caramelized nuts – do you like the sound of that? Port is the classic dark sweet wine, and it comes in several styles, from basic ruby, to tawny, matured in cask for 10 years or more, to vintage, which matures to mellowness in the bottle. The Portuguese island of Madeira produces fortified wines with rich brown smoky flavours and a startling bite of acidity: the sweet styles to look for are Bual and Malmsey. Decent sweet sherries are rare; oloroso dulce is a style with stunningly concentrated flavours. In southern France, Banyuls and Maury are deeply fruity fortified wines. Marsala, from Sicily, has rich brown sugar flavours with a refreshing sliver of acidity. The versatile Muscat grape makes luscious golden wines all around the Mediterranean, but also pops up in orange, black, and the gloriously rich, treacly brown versions that Australia does superbly.

• Port
• Bual and Malmsey Madeira
• Marsala
• Rich, sweet sherry styles include Pedro Ximénez, oloroso dulce
• Vins doux naturels from southern France: Banyuls, Maury
• Fortified (liqueur) Muscat 'stickies' from Australia

Buying for the long term

Most of this book is about wines to drink more or less immediately – that's how modern wines are made, and that's what you'll find in most High Street retail outlets. If you're looking for a mature vintage of a great wine that's ready to drink – or are prepared to wait 10 years or more for a great vintage to reach its peak – specialist wine merchants will be able to help; the Internet's another good place to look for mature wines. Here's my beginners' guide to buying wine for drinking over the longer term.

Auctions

A wine sale catalogue from one of the UK's auction houses will have wine enthusiasts drooling over names they certainly don't see every day. Better still, the lots are often of mature vintages that are ready to drink. Before you go, find out all you can about the producer and vintages described in the catalogue. My annually updated *Pocket Wine Book* is a good place to start, or *Michael Broadbent's Vintage Wines* for old and rare wines; the national wine magazines (*Decanter*, *Wine & Spirit*) run regular features on wine regions and their vintages. You can also learn a lot from tutored tastings – especially 'vertical' tastings, which compare different vintages. This is important – some merchants take the opportunity to clear inferior vintages at auction.

The drawbacks? You have no guarantee that the wine has been well stored, and if it's faulty you have little chance of redress. As prices of the most sought-after wines have soared, so it has become profitable either to forge the bottles and their contents or to try to pass off stock that is clearly out of condition. But for expensive and mature wines, I have to say that the top auction houses make a considerable effort to check the provenance and integrity of the wines. Don't forget that there will usually be a commission, or buyers' premium, to pay, so check out the small print in the sale catalogue. Online wine auctions have similar pros and cons.

If you've never bought wine at an auction before, a good place to start would be a local auctioneer such as Straker Chadwick in Abergavenny (tel: 01873 852624, www.strakerchadwick.co.uk) or Morphets in Harrogate (tel: 01423 530030, www.morphets.co.uk); they're less intimidating than the famous London houses of Christie's and Sotheby's and you may come away with some really exciting wine.

Buying en primeur

En primeur is a French term for wine which is sold before it is bottled, sometimes referred to as a 'future'. In the spring after the vintage the Bordeaux châteaux – and a few other wine-producing regions – hold tastings of barrel samples for members of the international wine trade. The châteaux then offer a proportion of their production to the wine merchants (négociants) in Bordeaux, who in turn offer it to wine merchants around the world at an opening price.

The advantage to the châteaux is that their capital is not tied up in expensive stock for the next year or two, until the wines are bottled and ready to ship. Traditionally merchants would buy en primeur for stock to be sold later at a higher price, while offering their customers the chance to take advantage of the opening prices as well. The idea of private individuals investing rather than institutions took off with a series of good Bordeaux vintages in the 1980s; it's got ever more hectic since then.

Wine for the future

There is a lot to be said for buying en primeur. For one thing, in a great vintage you may be able to find the finest and rarest wines far more cheaply than they will ever appear again. This was especially true of the 1990 vintage in Bordeaux; this, in turn, primed the market for the exceptional vintages of 1999 in Burgundy and 2000 in Bordeaux. Equally, when a wine – even a relatively inexpensive one – is made in very limited quantities, buying en primeur may be practically your only chance of getting hold of it.

In the past, British wine merchants and their privileged customers were able to 'buy double what you want, sell half for double what you paid, and drink for free', but as the market has opened up to people more interested in making a quick buck than drinking fine wine, the whole process has become more risky.

Another potential hazard is that a tasting assessment is difficult at an early date. There is a well-founded suspicion that many barrel samples are doctored (legally) to appeal to the most powerful consumer critics, in particular the American Robert Parker and the *Wine Spectator* magazine. The wine that is finally bottled may or may not bear a resemblance to what was tasted in the spring following the vintage. In any case, most serious red wines are in a difficult stage of their evolution in the spring, and with the best will in the world it is possible to get one's evaluation wrong. However, the aforementioned Americans, and magazines like *Decanter* and *Wine & Spirit*, will do their best to offer you accurate judgements on the newly offered wines, and most merchants who make a primeur offer also write a good assessment of the wines. You will find that many of them quote the Parker or *Wine Spectator* marks. Anything over 90 out of 100 risks being hyped and hiked in price. Many of the best bargains get marks between 85 and 89, since the 90+ marks are generally awarded for power rather than subtlety. Consideration can be given to the producer's reputation for consistency and to the general vintage assessment for the region.

Prices can go down as well as up. They may not increase significantly for some years after the campaign.

Some popular vintages are offered at ridiculously high prices – some unpopular ones too. It's only about twice a decade that the combination of high quality and fair prices offers the private buyer a chance of a good, guaranteed profit. Interestingly, if one highly-touted vintage is followed by another, the prices for the second one often have to fall because the market simply will not accept two inflated price structures in a row. Recent Bordeaux examples of this are the excellent 1990 after the much hyped 1989 and the potentially fine 2001 after the understandably hyped 2000.

2004 was a bigger, more classic, but more erratic vintage than 2003 in Bordeaux; the good news is that prices dropped by a third. A lot of people didn't buy the 2004 – and it was overshadowed by the 2005 – but don't overlook it: there's some absolutely smashing stuff at very reasonable prices.

The superlative 2005 vintage is certainly one of the best ever – but prices are some of the highest ever.

2006 is a much more patchy vintage, though some very tasty stuff was made (see box, right). Prices are well down on 2005, but still historically high.

Secure cellarage
Another worry is that the merchant you buy the wine from may not still be around to deliver it to you two years later. Buy from a merchant you trust, with a solid trading base in other wines.

Once the wines are shipped you may want your merchant to store the wine for you; there is usually a small charge for this. If your merchant offers cellarage, you should insist that (1) you receive a stock certificate; (2) your wines are stored separately from the merchant's own stocks; and (3) your cases are identifiable as your property and are labelled accordingly. All good merchants offer these safeguards as a minimum service.

Check the small print
Traditional wine merchants may quote prices exclusive of VAT and/or duty: wine may not be the bargain it first appears.

A wine quoted en primeur is usually offered on an ex-cellars (EC) basis; the price excludes shipping, duties and taxes such as VAT. A price quoted in bond (IB) in the UK includes shipping, but excludes duties and taxes. Duty paid (DP) prices exclude VAT. You should check beforehand the exact terms of sale with your merchant, who will give you a projection of the final 'duty paid delivered' price.

Clarke's canny picks

2005 is being hyped to the skies: it's an excellent vintage, but prices are sky-high. Now's a good time to think about investing in some 2006 red Bordeaux; the following make good, affordable stuff.

- Château Batailley (Pauillac)
- Château Cantenac Brown (Margaux)
- Château Ferrière (Margaux)
- Château Feytit-Clinet (Pomerol)
- Château Grand-Puy-Lacoste (Pauillac)
- Château Gruaud Larose (St-Julien)
- Château Haut-Bages Libéral (Pauillac)
- Château Langoa Barton (St-Julien)
- Château Monbrison (Margaux)
- Château les Ormes de Pez (St-Estèphe)
- Château Pibran (Pauillac)
- Château Poujeaux (Moulis)
- Château Siran (Margaux)
- Château Sociando-Mallet (Haut-Médoc)
- Château du Tertre (Margaux)

Retailers' directory

All these retailers have been chosen on the basis of the quality and interest of their lists. If you want to find a local retailer, turn to the Who's Where directory on page 192.

The following services are available where indicated:
C = cellarage **G** = glass hire/loan **M** = mail/online order **T** = tastings and talks

A & B Vintners

Little Tawsden, Spout Lane, Brenchley, Kent TN12 7AS (01892) 724977
fax (01892) 722673 e-mail info@abvintners.co.uk website www.abvintners.co.uk
hours Mon–Fri 9–6 cards MasterCard, Visa delivery Free 5 cases or more, otherwise £11.75 per consignment UK mainland minimum order 1 mixed case en primeur Burgundy, Languedoc, Rhône. C M T
❂ Specialists in Burgundy, the Rhône and southern France, with a string of top-quality domaines from all three regions.

Adnams

head office & mail order Sole Bay Brewery, Southwold, Suffolk IP18 6JW (01502) 727222
fax (01502) 727223 e-mail wines@adnams.co.uk website www.adnamswines.co.uk
shops Adnams Wine Cellar & Kitchen Store, Victoria Street, Southwold, Suffolk IP18 6JW • Adnams Wine Shop, Pinkney's Lane, Southwold, Suffolk IP18 6EW • Adnams Wine Cellar & Kitchen Store, The Old School House, Park Road, Holkham, Wells-next-the-Sea, Norfolk NR23 1AB (01328) 711714 • Adnams Wine Cellar & Kitchen Store, Station Road, Woodbridge, Suffolk IP12 4AU (01394) 386594 • Adnams Wine Cellar & Kitchen Store, Bath Row Warehouse, St Mary's Passage, Stamford, Lincolnshire PE9 2HG (01780) 753127 hours (Orderline) Mon–Fri 9–6.30, Sat 9–5; Wine Cellar & Kitchen Store Southwold: Mon–Sat 9–6, Sun 11–4; Wine Cellar & Kitchen Store Holkham, Woodbridge and Stamford: Mon–Sat 10–6, Sun 11–4; Wine Shop Southwold: Mon–Sat 9.30–5.30, Sun 11–4 cards Maestro, MasterCard, Visa, Delta discounts 5% for 5 cases or more delivery Free for orders over £125 in most of mainland UK, otherwise £7.50 en primeur Bordeaux, Burgundy, Chile, Rhône, Southern France
❂ Extensive list of personality-packed wines from around the world, chosen by Adnams' enthusiastic team of buyers – so there are wines you won't find anywhere else.

Aldi Stores

PO Box 26, Atherstone, Warwickshire CV9 2SH; 320 stores

store location line 08705 134262   website www.aldi-stores.co.uk   hours Mon–Wed 9–6, Thurs–Fri 9–7, Sat 8.30–5.30, Sun 10–4 (selected stores)   cards Maestro, Visa (debit only)

✪ *Decent everyday stuff from around the world, with lots of wines around £3.*

armit

5 Royalty Studios, 105 Lancaster Road, London W11 1QF (020) 7908 0600

fax (020) 7908 0601   e-mail info@armit.co.uk   website www.armit.co.uk   hours Mon–Fri 9–5.30 cards Maestro, MasterCard, Visa   delivery Free for orders over £180, otherwise £15 delivery charge minimum order 1 case   en primeur Bordeaux, Burgundy, Italy, Rhône, New World. C M T

✪ *Particularly strong on wines to go with food – they supply some of the country's top restaurants.*

ASDA

head office Asda House, Southbank, Great Wilson Street, Leeds LS11 5AD (0113) 243 5435 fax (0113) 241 8666 customer service (0500) 100055; 320 stores website www.asda.co.uk hours Selected stores open 24 hrs, see local store for details cards Maestro, MasterCard, Visa T

✪ *Good-value basics – lots under a fiver – and the range now includes some interesting wines at £7+.*

L'Assemblage Fine Wine Traders

Pallant Court, 10 West Pallant, Chichester, West Sussex PO19 1TG (01243) 537775

fax (01243) 538644 e-mail sales@lassemblage.co.uk website www.lassemblage.co.uk hours Mon–Fri 9.30–6 cards Maestro, MasterCard, Visa delivery Free for orders over £500 minimum order 1 mixed case or by arrangement en primeur Bordeaux, Burgundy, Port, Rhône. C M T

✪ *Specialist in one-off cases of fine, mature wine – great for special anniversaries.*

Averys Wine Merchants

4 High Street, Nailsea, Bristol BS48 1BT (01275) 811100

fax (01275) 811101 e-mail sales@averys.com website www.averys.com

• Shop and Cellars, 9 Culver Street, Bristol BS1 5LD (0117) 921 4146 fax (0117) 922 6318 e-mail cellars@averys.com hours Mon–Fri 9–7, Sat 9.30–5.30, Sun 10–4; Shop Mon–Sat 9–7 cards AmEx, Maestro, MasterCard, Visa discounts Monthly mail order offers, Discover Wine with Averys 13th bottle free

delivery £5.99 per delivery address en primeur Bordeaux, Burgundy, Port, Rhône. C G M T
✿ *A small but very respectable selection from just about everywhere in France, Italy, Spain and Germany, as well as some good New World wines.*

Bacchus Wine

38 Market Place, Olney, Bucks MK46 4AJ (01234) 711140
fax (01234) 711199 e-mail wine@bacchus.co.uk website www.bacchus.co.uk
hours Mon 12–7, Tue–Fri 10.30–7, Sat 9.30–6, Sun 12–4 cards AmEx, Diners, Maestro, MasterCard, Visa
delivery £5 per dozen, local only minimum order 1 case. G M T
✿ *France and Italy have the broadest coverage, but there are some gems from Argentina, Australia, Austria and South Africa – and you'll find many wines under £10.*

Ballantynes Wine Merchants

211–17 Cathedral Road, Cardiff CF11 9PP (02920) 222202
fax (02920) 222112 e-mail richard@ballantynes.co.uk website www.ballantynes.co.uk
hours Mon–Fri 9.30–6.30, Sat 9.30–5.30 cards Access, Maestro, MasterCard, Visa discounts 8% per case
delivery £9.99 for first case; £4.99 for subsequent cases en primeur Bordeaux, Burgundy, Italy, Rhône. C G M T
✿ *Italy, Burgundy, Rhône and Languedoc-Roussillon are stunning, most regions of France are well represented and there's some terrific stuff from Australia, New Zealand and Spain.*

Balls Brothers

313 Cambridge Heath Road, London E2 9LQ (020) 7739 1642
fax 0870 243 9775 direct sales (020) 7739 1642 e-mail wine@ballsbrothers.co.uk
website www.ballsbrothers.co.uk hours Mon–Fri 9–5.30 cards AmEx, Diners, Maestro, MasterCard, Visa
delivery Free 1 case or more locally; £8 1 case, free 2 cases or more, England, Wales and Scottish Lowlands; islands and Scottish Highlands phone for details. G M T
✿ *French specialist – you'll find something of interest from most regions – with older vintages available. Spain and Australia are also very good. Many of the wines can be enjoyed in Balls Brothers' London wine bars and restaurants.*

H & H Bancroft Wines

1 China Wharf, 29 Mill Street, London SE1 2BQ (020) 7232 5450
fax (020) 7232 5451 e-mail sales@bancroftwines.com website www.bancroftwines.com

hours Mon–Fri 9–5.30 cards Delta, Maestro, MasterCard, Visa discounts Negotiable
delivery £15 for 1–2 cases in mainland UK; free 3 cases or more or for an order value of £300 or more.
minimum order 1 unmixed case en primeur Bordeaux, Burgundy, Rhône. C M T
✪ *Bancroft are UK agents for an impressive flotilla of French winemakers: Burgundy, Rhône, Loire and some interesting wines from southern France. Italy looks promising, too.*

Bat & Bottle

office The Treehouse, 9 Ashwell Road, Oakham LE15 6QG (01572) 759735
warehouse 24d Pillings Road, Oakham LE15 6QF fax 0870 458 2505 e-mail post@batwine.co.uk
website www.batwine.co.uk hours Warehouse: Sat 9–2. Please call to arrange an appointment outside these hours
cards Maestro, MasterCard, Visa delivery Free for orders over £150 G M T
✪ *Ben and Emma Robson specialize in Italy, and in characterful wines from small producers discovered on their regular visits to the country.*

Bennetts Fine Wines

High Street, Chipping Campden, Glos GL55 6AG (01386) 840392
fax (01386) 840974 e-mail enquiries@bennettsfinewines.com website www.bennettsfinewines.com
hours Tues–Sat 9.30–6 cards Access, Maestro, MasterCard, Visa discounts On collected orders of 1 case or more
delivery £6 per case, minimum charge £12, free for orders over £200 en primeur Burgundy, California, Rhône, New Zealand. G M T
✪ *Reasonable prices for high-calibre producers – there's lots to choose from at around £10. Mainly from France and Italy, but some good German, Spanish and Portuguese wines, too.*

Berkmann Wine Cellars

10–12 Brewery Road, London N7 9NH (020) 7609 4711 fax (020) 7607 0018 e-mail orders@berkmann.co.uk
• Brunel Park, Vincients Road, Bumpers Farm, Chippenham, Wiltshire SN14 6NQ (01249) 463501
fax (01249) 463502 e-mail orders.chippenham@berkmann.co.uk
• Brian Coad Wine Cellars, 41b Valley Road, Plympton, Plymouth, Devon PL7 1RF (01752) 334970 fax (01752) 346540
e-mail orders.briancoad@berkmann.co.uk
• Pagendam Pratt Wine Cellars, 16 Marston Moor Business Park, Rudgate, Tockwith, North Yorkshire YO26 7QF

The following services are available where indicated: C = cellarage G = glass hire/loan M = mail/online order T = tastings and talks

(01423) 337567 fax (01423) 357568 e-mail orders@pagendampratt.co.uk

• T M Robertson Wine Cellars, Unit 12, A1 Industrial Estate, 232 Sir Harry Lauder Road, Portobello, Edinburgh EH15 2QA
(0131) 657 6390 fax (0131) 657 6389 e-mail orders@tmrobertson.co.uk

• Churchill Vintners, 401 Walsall Road, Perry Bar, Birmingham B42 1BT (0121) 356 8888
fax (0121) 356 1111 e-mail info@churchill-vintners.co.uk
website www.berkmann.co.uk hours Mon–Fri 9–5.30 cards Maestro, MasterCard, Visa
discounts £3 per unmixed case collected delivery Free for orders over £120 to UK mainland (excluding the Highlands)
minimum order 1 mixed case. C G M

✪ As the UK agent for, among others, Antinori, Maculan, Mastroberardino, Masi and Tasca d'Almerita, there are some great
Italian wines here. An incredibly diverse list including wines from Mexico, Corsica and India.

Berry Bros. & Rudd

3 St James's Street, London SW1A 1EG (020) 7396 9600
fax (020) 7396 9611 orders office 0870 900 4300 (lines open Mon–Fri 9–6 orders fax 0870 900 4301
• Berrys' Factory Outlet, Hamilton Close, Houndmills, Basingstoke, Hampshire RG21 6YB (01256) 323566
e-mail orders@bbr.com website www.bbr.com hours St James's Street: Mon–Fri 10–6, Sat 10–5; Berrys' Factory
Outlet: Mon–Fri 10–6, Sat–Sun 10–4 cards AmEx, Diners, Maestro, MasterCard, Visa discounts Variable
delivery Free for orders of £200 or more, otherwise £10 en primeur Bordeaux, Burgundy, Rhône. C G M T

✪ The Blue List covers old, rare fine wines while the main list is both classy and wide-ranging. There's an emphasis on the
classic regions of France. Berry's Own Selection is extensive, with wines made by world-class producers.

Bibendum Wine Limited

mail order 113 Regents Park Road, London NW1 8UR (020) 7449 4120
fax (020) 7449 4121 e-mail sales@bibendum-wine.co.uk website www.bibendum-wine.co.uk
hours Mon–Fri 9–6 cards Maestro, MasterCard, Visa delivery Free throughout mainland UK for orders over £250,
otherwise £15 en primeur Bordeaux, Burgundy, New World, Rhône, Port. M T

✪ Equally strong in the Old World and the New: Huet in Vouvray and Lageder in Alto Adige are matched by d'Arenberg and
Katnook from Australia and Catena Zapata from Argentina.

Big Red Wine Company

mail order Barton Coach House, The Street, Barton Mills, Suffolk IP28 6AA (01638) 510803
e-mail sales@bigredwine.co.uk website www.bigredwine.co.uk hours Mon–Sat 9–6

cards AmEx, Delta, Maestro, Mastercard, Visa, PayPal discounts 5–15% for Wine Club members and on occasional offers; minimum £3 unmixed case discount; discounts for large orders negotiable delivery £5 per consignment for orders under £150, £10 for orders under £50, UK mainland en primeur Bordeaux, Rhône. C G M T

✪ *Intelligently chosen, reliably individualistic wines from well-established growers in France. A list worth reading, full of information and provocative opinion – and they're not overcharging.*

Booths Supermarkets

E H Booth & Co, Booths Central Office, Longridge Road, Ribbleton, Preston PR2 5BX (01772) 693800
fax (01772) 693893; 26 stores across the North of England
website www.booths.co.uk and www.booths-wine.co.uk
hours Office: Mon–Fri 8.30–5; shop hours vary cards AmEx, Electron, Maestro, MasterCard, Solo, Visa
discounts 5% off any 6 bottles. G T

✪ *A list for any merchant to be proud of, never mind a supermarket. There's plenty around £5, but if you're prepared to hand over £7–9 you'll find some really interesting stuff.*

Bordeaux Index

6th Floor, 159–173 St John Street, London EC1V 4QJ (020) 7253 2110
fax (020) 7490 1955 e-mail sales@bordeauxindex.com website www.bordeauxindex.com
hours Mon–Fri 8.30–6 cards AmEx, Maestro, MasterCard, Visa, JCB (transaction fees apply)
delivery (private sales only) free for orders over £2,000 UK mainland; others at cost minimum order £500
en primeur Bordeaux, Burgundy, Rhône, Italy. C T

✪ *An extensive list for big spenders, with pages and pages of red Bordeaux. You'll also find top Burgundies and Rhônes, and some interesting stuff from Italy, Australia and America.*

Budgens Stores

head office Musgrave House, Widewater Place, Moorhall Road, Harefield, Uxbridge, Middlesex UB9 6NS 0870 050 0158
fax 0870 050 0159, 210 stores mainly in southern England and East Anglia – for nearest store call 0800 526002
e-mail info@ budgens.co.uk website www.budgens.co.uk
hours vary according to size and location (55 stores open 24 hours); usually Mon–Sat 8–8, Sun 10–4
cards Maestro, MasterCard, Solo, Visa. G

✪ *These days you can be reasonably confident of going into a Budgens store and coming out with something you'd actually like to drink, at bargain-basement prices upwards.*

The Butlers Wine Cellar

247 Queens Park Road, Brighton BN2 9XJ (01273) 698724

fax (01273) 622761 e-mail henry@butlers-winecellar.co.uk website www.butlers-winecellar.co.uk

hours Tue–Sat 11–7 cards Access, AmEx, Maestro, MasterCard, Visa delivery Free locally 1 case or more; free UK mainland 3 cases or more en primeur Bordeaux. G M T

✪ Henry Butler personally chooses all the wines on the regular list and there is some fascinating stuff there, including English wines from local growers such as Breaky Bottom. The bin ends include some mature claret for a tenner or less – check the website or join the mailing list as offers change regularly.

Anthony Byrne

mail order Ramsey Business Park, Stocking Fen Road, Ramsey, Cambs PE26 2UR (01487) 814555

fax (01487) 814962 e-mail anthony@abfw.co.uk or tim@abfw.co.uk website www.abfw.co.uk

hours Mon–Fri 9–5.30 cards MasterCard, Visa discounts available on cases delivery Free 5 cases or more, or orders of £250 or more; otherwise £12 minimum order 1 case en primeur Bordeaux, Burgundy, Rhône. C M T

✪ A serious range of Burgundy; smaller but focused lists from Bordeaux and the Rhône; carefully selected wines from Alsace, Loire and Provence; and increasing coverage of South Africa.

D Byrne & Co

Victoria Buildings, 12 King Street, Clitheroe, Lancashire BB7 2EP (01200) 423152

hours Mon–Sat 8.30–6 cards Maestro, MasterCard, Visa delivery Free within 50 miles; nationally £20 1st case, £5 subsequent cases en primeur Bordeaux, Burgundy, Rhône, Germany. G M T

✪ One of northern England's best wine merchants, with a hugely impressive range. Mature clarets, stacks of Burgundy, faultless Loire and Rhône, and many, many more, both Old and New World. I urge you to go see for yourself.

Cape Wine and Food

77 Laleham Road, Staines, Middlesex TW18 2EA (01784) 451860

fax (01784) 469267 e-mail ross@capewineandfood.com website www.capewineandfood.com

hours Mon–Sat 10–6, Sun 10–5 cards AmEx, Maestro, MasterCard, Visa discounts 10% mixed case. G M T

✪ If you're looking for South African wine, this shop is the place to visit. Alongside wines for everyday drinking, there are some of the Cape's top red blends, going up to around £50 a bottle.

Les Caves de Pyrene

Pew Corner, Old Portsmouth Road, Artington, Guildford GU3 1LP (office) (01483) 538820 (shop) (01483) 554750
fax (01483) 455068 e-mail sales@lescaves.co.uk website www.lescaves.co.uk
hours Mon–Fri 9–5 cards Maestro, MasterCard, Visa delivery Free for orders over £180 within M25, elsewhere at cost
discounts negotiable minimum order 1 mixed case en primeur South-West France. G M T
✪ *Excellent operation, devoted to seeking out top wines from all over southern France. Other areas of France are looking increasingly good too, Italy's regions are well represented, and there's some choice stuff from New Zealand.*

ChateauOnline

mail order BP68, 39602 Arbois Cedex, France (0033) 3 84 66 42 21
fax (0033) 1 55 30 31 41 customer service 0800 169 2736 website www.chateauonline.com
hours Mon–Fri 8–11.30, 12.30–4.30 cards AmEx, Maestro, MasterCard, Visa
delivery £7.99 per consignment en primeur Bordeaux, Burgundy, Languedoc-Roussillon.
✪ *French specialist, with an impressive list of over 2000 wines. Easy-to-use website with a well-thought-out range of mixed cases, frequent special offers and bin end sales.*

Cockburns of Leith (incorporating J E Hogg)

Cockburn House, Unit 3, Abbeyhill Industrial Estate, Abbey Lane, Edinburgh EH8 8HL (0131) 661 8400
fax (0131) 661 7333 e-mail sales@cockburnsofleith.co.uk
website www.cockburnsofleith.co.uk hours Mon–Fri 9–6; Sat 10–5 cards Maestro, MasterCard, Visa
delivery Free 12 or more bottles within Edinburgh; elsewhere £7 1–2 cases, free 3 cases or more
en primeur Bordeaux, Burgundy. G T
✪ *Clarets at bargain prices – in fact wines from all over France, including plenty of vins de pays. Among other countries New Zealand looks promising, and there's a great range of sherries.*

Connolly's Wine Merchants

Arch 13, 220 Livery Street, Birmingham B3 1EU (0121) 236 9269/3837
fax (0121) 233 2339 e-mail sales@connollyswine.co.uk website www.connollyswine.co.uk
hours Mon–Fri 9–5.30, except Thurs 9–7, Sat 10–4 cards AmEx, Maestro, MasterCard, Visa
delivery Surcharge outside Birmingham area discounts 10% for cash & carry en primeur Burgundy. G M T
✪ *There's something for everyone here. Burgundy, Bordeaux and the Rhône all look very good; and there are top names from Germany, Italy, Spain and California. Monthly tutored tastings and winemaker dinners.*

The Co-operative Group

head office New Century House, Manchester M60 4ES Freephone 0800 068 6727 for stock details; approx. 3,000 licensed stores e-mail customer_relations@co-op.co.uk website www.co-op.co.uk hours Variable cards Variable

✪ Champions of Fairtrade and organic wines. Tasty stuff from South Africa, Australia, Chile and Argentina for around £5.

Corney & Barrow

head office No. 1 Thomas More Street, London E1W 1YZ (020) 7265 2400 fax (020) 7265 2539

• 194 Kensington Park Road, London W11 2ES (020) 7221 5122

• Corney & Barrow East Anglia, Belvoir House, High Street, Newmarket CB8 8DH (01638) 600000

• Corney & Barrow (Scotland) with Whighams of Ayr, 8 Academy Street, Ayr KA7 1HT (01292) 267000, and Oxenfoord Castle, by Pathhead, Mid Lothian EH37 5UD (01875) 321921

e-mail wine@corbar.co.uk website www.corneyandbarrow.com hours Mon–Fri 8–6 (24-hr answering machine); Kensington Mon–Fri 10.30–9, Sat 9.30–8; Newmarket Mon–Sat 9–6; Edinburgh Mon–Fri 9–6; Ayr Mon–Fri 9–6, Sat 9.30–5.30 cards AmEx, Maestro, MasterCard, Visa delivery Free 24 or more bottles within M25 boundary, elsewhere free 36 or more bottles or for orders above £200. Otherwise £9 + VAT per delivery. For Scotland and East Anglia, please contact the relevant office en primeur Bordeaux, Burgundy, Champagne, Rhône, Italy, Spain. C G M T

✪ Top names in French and other European wines; Australia, South Africa and South America also impressive. Wines in every price bracket – try them out at Corney & Barrow wine bars in London.

Croque-en-Bouche

Groom's Cottage, Underdown, Gloucester Road, Ledbury HR8 2JE (01531) 636400

fax 08707 066282 e-mail mail@croque-en-bouche.co.uk website www.croque-en-bouche.co.uk hours By appointment 7 days a week cards MasterCard, Visa, debit cards discounts 3% for orders over £500 if paid by cheque or debit card delivery Free locally; elsewhere £5 per consignment; free in England and Wales for orders over £500 if paid by credit card minimum order 1 mixed case (12 items) or £180 M

✪ A wonderful list, including older wines. Mature Australian reds from the 1990s; terrific stuff from the Rhône; some top clarets; and a generous sprinkling from other parts of the world.

DeFINE Food & Wine

Chester Road, Sandiway, Cheshire CW8 2NH (01606) 882101

fax (01606) 888407 e-mail office@definefoodandwine.com website www.definefoodandwine.com hours Mon–Sat 10–8; Sun 12–6 cards AmEx, Maestro, MasterCard, Visa discounts 5% off 12 bottles or more delivery Free locally, otherwise £10 UK minimum order 1 mixed case. C G M T

✪ *Wine shop and delicatessen, with British cheeses and food from Italy and Spain. Excellent, if conservative stuff from Bordeaux and the Loire; less conservative choices from elsewhere.*

Devigne Wines

211 The Murrays, Edinburgh EH17 8UN (0131) 644 9058

Fax (05600) 756 287 e-mail info@devignewines.co.uk website www.devignewines.co.uk hours Mon–Fri 10–6 (telephone 7 days) cards Maestro, MasterCard, Visa discounts selected mixed cases at introductory rate delivery free for orders over £300, otherwise £6.50 per consignment M

✪ *Small list specializing in French wine: traditional method sparkling wines from all over France, a wide choice of rosés, red Gaillac from the South-West and a range of Languedoc reds.*

Direct Wine Shipments

5–7 Corporation Square, Belfast, Northern Ireland BT1 3AJ (028) 9050 8000

fax (028) 9050 8004 e-mail shop@directwine.co.uk website www.directwine.co.uk hours Mon–Fri 9–6.30 (Thur 10–8), Sat 9.30–5.30 cards Access, Maestro, MasterCard, Visa discounts 10% in the form of complementary wine with each case delivery Free Northern Ireland 1 case or more, variable delivery charge for UK mainland depending on customer spend en primeur Bordeaux, Burgundy, Rhône. C M T

✪ *Rhône, Spain, Australia and Burgundy outstanding; Italy, Germany and Chile not far behind; there's good stuff from pretty much everywhere. Wine courses, tastings and expert advice offered.*

Nick Dobson Wines

38 Crail Close, Wokingham, Berkshire RG41 2PZ 0800 849 3078

fax 0870 460 2358 e-mail nick.dobson@nickdobsonwines.co.uk website www.nickdobsonwines.co.uk hours Mon–Sat 9–5 cards Access, Maestro, MasterCard, Visa delivery £7 + VAT 1 case; £5.50 + VAT 2nd case and subsequent cases to UK mainland addresses. Free local delivery. M T

✪ *Mail order outfit specializing in wines from Switzerland, Austria and Beaujolais. Burgundy, Germany and New Zealand are also covered in this list. Plenty of wines at under £10.*

Domaine Direct

8 Cynthia Street, London N1 9JF (020) 7837 1142

fax (020) 7837 8605 e-mail mail@domainedirect.co.uk website www.domainedirect.co.uk

hours 8.30–6 or answering machine cards Maestro, MasterCard, Visa delivery Free London; elsewhere in UK mainland 1 case £12, 2 cases £16.90, or more free minimum order 1 mixed case en primeur Burgundy. M T
✪ *Sensational Burgundy list; prices are very reasonable for the quality. Also the Burgundian-style Chardonnays from Australia's Leeuwin Estate.*

Farr Vintners

220 Queenstown Road, Battersea, London SW8 4LP (020) 7821 2000
fax (020) 7821 2020 e-mail sales@farrvintners.com website www.farrvintners.com
hours Mon–Fri 10–6 cards Access, Maestro, Mastercard, Visa delivery London £1 per case (min £14); elsewhere at cost minimum order £500 + VAT en primeur Bordeaux. C M T
✪ *A fantastic list of the world's finest wines. The majority is Bordeaux, but you'll also find top stuff and older vintages of white Burgundy, red Rhône, plus Italy, Australia and California.*

Fine Wines of New Zealand

mail order PO Box 476, London NW5 2NZ (020) 7482 0093
fax (020) 7267 8400 e-mail sales@fwnz.co.uk or info@fwnz.co.uk website www.fwnz.co.uk
hours Mon–Sat 9–6 cards Access, Maestro, MasterCard, Visa discounts 6 or more cases
delivery Free for 1 mixed case or more UK mainland minimum order 1 mixed case. M
✪ *There are some great names from New Zealand, including Ata Rangi, Hunter's, Kumeu River, Pegasus Bay and Stonyridge.*

Irma Fingal-Rock

64 Monnow Street, Monmouth NP25 3EN
tel & fax 01600 712372 e-mail tom@pinotnoir.co.uk website www.pinotnoir.co.uk
hours Mon 9.30–1.30, Thurs & Fri 9.30–5.30, Sat 9.30–5 cards Maestro, MasterCard, Visa discounts 5% for at least 12 bottles collected from shop, 7.5% for collected orders over £500, 10% for collected orders over £1,200 delivery Free locally (within 30 miles); orders further afield free if over £100. G M T
✪ *The list's great strength is Burgundy, from some very good growers and priced between £6 and £40. Small but tempting selections from other French regions, as well as Italy, Spain, Portugal and the New World.*

The following services are available where indicated: C = cellarage **G** = glass hire/loan **M** = mail/online order **T** = tastings and talks

Flagship Wines

417 Hatfield Road, St Albans, Hertfordshire AL4 0XP (01727) 865309 e-mail sales@flagshipwines.co.uk
website www.flagshipwines.co.uk hours Tues–Thurs 11–6, Fri 11–7.30, Sat 10–6 cards AmEx, Maestro,
MasterCard, Visa delivery Free to St Albans addresses and £7.50 to other UK mainland addresses. G M T
✪ *Well-run independent whose prices can match those of the supermarkets – and you get the friendly, well-informed advice of boss Julia Jenkins thrown in. Some interesting Italians but strongest in Spain, Australia and Portugal.*

Le Fleming Wines

mail order 19 Spenser Road, Harpenden, Hertfordshire AL5 5NW (01582) 760125
e-mail cherry@ leflemingwines.co.uk website www.leflemingwines.co.uk hours 24-hour answering machine
discounts 5% on large orders delivery Free locally minimum order 1 case. G
✪ *Mainly New World and France, alongside excellent Australian and South African. List also includes short, focused selections from Italy and Spain.*

The Flying Corkscrew

Leighton Buzzard Road, Water End, Nr Hemel Hempstead, Hertfordshire HP1 3BD (01442) 412311
fax (01442) 412313 e-mail sales@flyingcorkscrew.co.uk website www.flyingcorkscrew.co.uk
hours Mon–Wed 10–7, Thurs–Fri 10–8, Sat 10–7, Sun 11–5 cards AmEx, Maestro, MasterCard, Visa
discounts 10% on case delivery Free for orders over £100; £10 per case under £100 G M T
✪ *Every corner of France has been explored, and the list is overflowing with an extensive and imaginative range of wines. But France is just the beginning: Italy, Australia and the US are terrific. Friendly, knowledgeable staff – and if you're local, look out for tastings led by experts and winemakers.*

Fortnum & Mason

181 Piccadilly, London W1A 1ER (020) 7734 8040
fax (020) 7437 3278 ordering line 0845 300 1707 e-mail info@fortnumandmason.co.uk
website www.fortnumandmason.com hours Mon–Sat 10–6.30, Sun 12–6 (Food Hall and Patio Restaurant only)
cards AmEx, Diners, Maestro, MasterCard, Visa discounts 1 free bottle per unmixed dozen
delivery £7 per delivery address en primeur Bordeaux. M T
✪ *Impressive names from just about everywhere, including Champagne, Bordeaux, Burgundy, Italy, Germany, Australia, New Zealand, South Africa and California. Impeccably sourced own-label range.*

Friarwood

26 New King's Road, London SW6 4ST (020) 7736 2628 fax (020) 7731 0411

• 16 Dock Street, Leith, Edinburgh, EH6 6EY (0131) 554 4159 fax (0131) 554 6703 e-mail sales@friarwood.com; edinburgh@friarwood.com website www.friarwood.com hours Mon–Sat 10–7
cards AmEx, Diners, Maestro, MasterCard, Visa, Solo, Electron discounts 5% on mixed cases, 10% unmixed
delivery (London) Free within M25 and on orders over £250 in mainland UK; (Edinburgh) free locally and for 2 cases or more elsewhere (under 2 cases at cost) en primeur Bordeaux. C G M T
✪ *The focus is Bordeaux, including mature wines from a good selection of petits châteaux as well as classed growths. Burgundy and other French regions are strong too.*

Gauntleys

4 High Street, Exchange Arcade, Nottingham NG1 2ET (0115) 911 0555

fax (0115) 911 0557 e-mail rhône@gauntleywine.com website www.gauntleywine.com
hours Mon–Sat 9–5.30 cards Maestro, MasterCard, Visa delivery Free within Nottingham area, otherwise 1–3 cases £9.50, 4 or more cases free minimum order 1 case en primeur Alsace, Burgundy, Italy, Loire, Rhône, southern France, Spain. M T
✪ *They've won awards for their Rhône and Alsace lists, but the Loire, Burgundy, southern France and Spain are all top-notch too.*

Goedhuis & Co

6 Rudolf Place, Miles Street, London SW8 1RP (020) 7793 7900

fax (020) 7793 7170 e-mail sales@goedhuis.com website www.goedhuis.com
hours Mon–Fri 9–5.30 cards Maestro, MasterCard, Visa delivery Free 3 cases or more, otherwise £15 England, elsewhere at cost minimum order 1 unmixed case en primeur Bordeaux, Burgundy, Rhône. C G M T
✪ *Fine wine specialist. Bordeaux, Burgundy and the Rhône are the core of the list, but everything is good.*

Great Northern Wine

The Warehouse, Blossomgate, Ripon, North Yorkshire HG4 2AJ (01765) 606767

fax (01765) 609151 e-mail info@greatnorthernwine.co.uk website www.greatnorthernwine.co.uk
hours Tues–Fri 9–6, Sat 9–5.30 cards AmEx, Maestro, MasterCard, Visa discounts 10% on case quantities
delivery Free locally, elsewhere at cost en primeur Bordeaux. G M T
✪ *Particular strengths here are Spain, New Zealand and South America.*

Great Western Wine

The Wine Warehouse, Wells Road, Bath BA2 3AP (01225) 322810 (shop) or (01225) 322800 (office)
fax (01225) 442139 e-mail retail@greatwesternwine.co.uk website www.greatwesternwine.co.uk
hours Mon–Fri 10–7, Sat 10–6 cards AmEx, Maestro, MasterCard, Visa discounts Negotiable
delivery £8.95 per case, free over £200 minimum order 1 mixed case en primeur Australia, Bordeaux, Burgundy,
Rioja. C G M T
✪ *Wide-ranging list, bringing in wines from individual growers around the world. Also organizes events and tastings.*

Peter Green & Co

37A/B Warrender Park Road, Edinburgh EH9 1HJ (0131) 229 5925
fax (0131) 229 0606 e-mail shop@petergreenwines.com hours Tues–Thur 10–6.30, Fri 10–7.30, Sat 10–6.30
cards Maestro, MasterCard, Visa discounts 5% on unmixed half-dozens delivery Free in Edinburgh
minimum order (For delivery) 1 case. G T
✪ *Extensive and adventurous list: Tunisia, India and the Lebanon rub shoulders with France, Italy and Germany.*

Green & Blue

36–38 Lordship Lane, East Dulwich, London, SE22 8HJ (020) 8693 9250
fax (020) 8693 9260 e-mail info@greenandbluewines.com website www.greenandbluewines.com
hours Shop: Mon–Fri 10–10pm, Sat 9am–11pm, Sun 12–10pm; Bar: Mon–Sat 9am–12am, Sun 12–11pm
cards Delta, Maestro, MasterCard, Visa discounts 5% on unmixed half-dozens delivery G T Free locally over £75,
otherwise £15; outside London dependent on weight, £10 under £150. G T
✪ *A tempting list full of unusual, intriguing wines you really want to drink – and you can try them on the spot, in the wine
bar, which serves tapas-style food. The staff are knowledgeable, and there's a waiting list for the popular tutored tastings.*

Halifax Wine Company

18 Prescott Street, Halifax, West Yorkshire HX1 2LG (01422) 256333
e-mail andy@halifaxwinecompany.com website www.halifaxwinecompany.com hours Tues–Fri 9.30–6, Sat 9–5.
Closed first week in January and first week in August. cards Access, Maestro, MasterCard, Visa discounts 8% on 12
bottles or more for personal callers to the shop delivery Free in West Yorkshire on orders over £75; rest of UK mainland
£4.95 for first 12 bottles then £2.95 per subsequent case. G M T
✪ *Exciting and wide-ranging list. They've won awards for their coverage of Spain and Portugal, but Australia and New
Zealand look good and other countries – including Greece – aren't neglected.*

Handford Wines

12 Portland Road, Holland Park, London W11 4LE (020) 7221 9614

• 105 Old Brompton Road, South Kensington, London SW7 3LE (020) 7589 6113 fax (020) 7581 2983
e-mail wine@handford.net website www.handford.net hours Mon–Sat 10–8.30 cards AmEx, MasterCard, Visa
discounts 5% on mixed cases delivery £8.25 for orders under £150 within UK en primeur Bordeaux. G M
✪ *Two delightful London shops, absolutely packed with the sort of wines I really want to drink.*

Roger Harris Wines

Loke Farm, Weston Longville, Norfolk NR9 5LG (01603) 880171
fax (01603) 880291 e-mail sales@rogerharriswines.co.uk website www.rogerharris wines.co.uk
hours Mon–Fri 9–5 cards AmEx, MasterCard, Visa delivery next working day UK mainland, £3 for orders up to £110, £2
up to £160, free over £160 minimum order 1 mixed case. M
✪ *Beaujolais-loving family business – Britain's acknowledged experts in this area.*

Harvey Nichols

109–125 Knightsbridge, London SW1X 7RJ (020) 7235 5000

• The Mailbox, 31–32 Wharfside Street, Birmingham B1 1RE (0121) 616 6000

• 30–34 St Andrew Square, Edinburgh EH2 3AD (0131) 524 8388

• 107–111 Briggate, Leeds LS1 6AZ (0113) 204 8888

• 21 New Cathedral Street, Manchester M3 1RE (0161) 828 8888

e-mail wineshop@harveynichols.com website www.harveynichols.com
hours (London) Mon–Fri 10–8, Sat 10–7, Sun 12–6 (Birmingham) Mon–Wed 10–6, Thurs 10–8, Fri–Sat 10–7, Sun 11–5
(Edinburgh) Mon–Wed 10–6, Thurs 10–8, Fri, Sat 10–7, Sun 11–5 (Leeds) Mon–Wed 10–6, Thurs–Fri 10–7, Sat 9–7,
Sun 12–6 (Manchester) Mon, Wed, Fri 10–7, Thurs 10–8, Sat 9–7, Sun 12–6 cards AmEx, Maestro, MasterCard, Visa.
✪ *Sought-after producers and cult wines, especially from France, Italy and California.*

Haynes Hanson & Clark

Sheep Street, Stow-on-the-Wold, Gloucestershire GL54 1AA (01451) 870808 fax (01451) 870508

• 7 Elystan Street, London SW3 3NT (020) 7584 7927 fax (020) 7584 7967

e-mail stow@hhandc.co.uk or london@hhandc.co.uk website www.hhandc.co.uk
hours (Stow) Mon–Fri 9–6, Sat 9–5.30 (London) Mon–Fri 9–7, Sat 9–4.30 cards Access, Maestro, MasterCard, Visa
discounts 10% unsplit case delivery Free central London and Gloucestershire for 1 case or more; elsewhere 1 case

£14.50, 2–3 cases £8.90 per case, 4 or more cases £7.25 per case, free orders for over £650
en primeur Bordeaux, Burgundy. M T
✪ *Known for its subtle, elegant wines: top-notch Burgundy is the main focus of the list, but other French regions are well represented, and there's interesting stuff from Spain, Italy, Australia and New Zealand.*

Hedley Wright

11 Twyford Centre, London Road, Bishop's Stortford, Herts CM23 3YT (01279) 465818 fax (01279) 465819
• Wyevale Garden Centre, Cambridge Road, Hitchin, Herts, SG4 0JT (01462) 431110 fax (01462) 422983
e-mail sales@hedleywright.co.uk website www.hedleywright.co.uk hours Mon–Wed 9–6, Thur–Fri 9–7, Sat 10–6; (Hitchin) Mon–Wed 11–7, Thur–Fri 11–8, Sat 11–7, Sun 11–5 cards AmEx, Maestro, MasterCard, Visa delivery £5 per delivery, free for orders over £100 minimum order 1 mixed case en primeur Bordeaux, Chile, Germany, Port. C G M T
✪ *A good all-round list, especially good for France and Italy.*

Hicks & Don

4 Old Station Yard, Edington, Westbury, Wiltshire BA13 4NT (01380) 831234 fax (01380) 831010
• Park House, North Elmham, Dereham, Norfolk NR20 5JY (01362) 668571 fax (01362) 668573
e-mail mailbox@hicksanddon.co.uk website www.hicksanddon.co.uk hours Mon–Fri 9–5 cards Maestro, MasterCard, Visa discounts Negotiable delivery Free over £100, otherwise £6 per case minimum order 1 case
en primeur Bordeaux, Burgundy, Chile, Italy, Port, Rhône. C G M T
✪ *Subtle, well-made wines that go with food and plenty of good-value wines at around £6 for everyday drinking.*

Jeroboams (incorporating Laytons)

head office 7–9 Elliot's Place, London N1 8HX (020) 7288 8888 fax (020) 7359 2616
shops 50–52 Elizabeth Street, London SW1W 9PB (020) 7730 8108
• 20 Davies Street, London W1K 3DT (020) 7499 1015
• 96 Holland Park Avenue, London W11 3RB (020) 7727 9359
• 6 Pont Street, London SW1X 9EL (020) 7235 1612
• 29 Heath Street, London NW3 6TR (020) 7435 6845
• 56 Walton Street, London SW3 1RB (020) 7589 2020
• 1 St. John's Wood High Street, London NW8 7NG (020) 7722 4020
• 13 Elgin Crescent, London W11 2JA (020) 7229 0527
• Mr Christian's Delicatessen, 11 Elgin Crescent, London W11 2JA (020) 7229 0501

• Milroy's of Soho, 3 Greek Street, London W1D 4NX (020) 7437 2385
e-mail sales@jeroboams.co.uk website www.jeroboams.co.uk
hours Offices Mon–Fri 9–6, shops Mon–Sat 9–7 (may vary) cards AmEx, Maestro, MasterCard, Visa
delivery Shops: free for orders of £50 or over in central London; mail order free for orders over £235, otherwise £15
delivery charge en primeur Bordeaux, Burgundy, Rhône. C G M T
✪ Concentrates on Burgundy, Rhône, Italy and Australia. Affordable and enjoyable wines. A wide range of fine foods,
especially cheeses and oilve oils, is available in the shops.

S H Jones
27 High Street, Banbury, Oxfordshire OX16 5EW (01295) 251179 fax (01295) 272352 e-mail banbury@shjones.com
• 9 Market Square, Bicester, Oxfordshire OX26 6AA (01869) 322448 e-mail bicester@shjones.com
• The Cellar Shop, 2 Riverside, Tramway Road, Banbury, Oxfordshire OX16 5TU (01295) 672296 fax (01295) 259560
e-mail retail@shjones.com
• 121 Regent Street, Leamington Spa, Warwickshire CV32 4NU (01926) 315609 e-mail leamington@shjones.com
website www.shjones.com hours Please call each store for details cards Maestro, MasterCard, Visa
delivery Free for 12 bottles of wine/spirits or total value over £100 within 15-mile radius of shops, otherwise £9.75 per
case en primeur Bordeaux, Burgundy, Port. C G M T
✪ Wide-ranging list with good Burgundies and Rhônes, clarets from under a tenner to top names and plenty of tasty stuff
from elsewhere – southern France to South America. There is now a wine bar at the High Street shop in Banbury.

Justerini & Brooks
mail order 61 St James's Street, London SW1A 1LZ (020) 7484 6400
fax (020) 7484 6499 e-mail justorders@justerinis.com website www.justerinis.com
hours Mon–Fri 9–5.30 cards AmEx, Maestro, MasterCard, Visa delivery Free for unmixed cases over £250, otherwise
£15 UK mainland minimum order 1 case en primeur Bordeaux, Burgundy, Italy, Rhône, Germany. C M T
✪ Superb list of top-quality wines from Europe's classic regions, as well as some excellent New World choices. While some
wines are very pricy, there is plenty for less than a tenner

Laithwaites
mail order New Aquitaine House, Exeter Way, Theale, Reading, Berkshire RG7 4PL order line 0870 444 8282
fax 0870 444 8182 e-mail orders@laithwaites.co.uk website www.laithwaites.co.uk hours 24-hr answering machine
cards AmEx, Diners, Maestro, MasterCard, Visa discounts On unmixed cases of 6 or 12 delivery £5.99 per order

en primeur Australia, Bordeaux, Burgundy, Port, Rhône, Rioja. C M T

✪ *Extensive selection of wines from France, Australia, Spain, Italy and elsewhere. Informative website offers excellent mixed cases, while the bin ends and special offers are good value.*

The Lay & Wheeler Group

Holton Park, Holton St Mary, Suffolk CO7 6NN 0845 330 1855

fax 0845 330 4095 e-mail sales@laywheeler.com website www.laywheeler.com

hours (order office) Mon–Fri 8.30–5.30, Sat 9–1 cards AmEx, Maestro, MasterCard, Visa delivery £9.95; free for orders over £200 en primeur Bordeaux, Burgundy, Port (some vintages), Rhône, Spain. C M T

• Wheeler Cellars, 117 Gosbecks Park, Colchester, Essex CO2 9JJ (01206) 713560 fax (01206) 769552 e-mail wheeler.cellars@laywheeler.com C G M T

✪ *There's enough first-class Bordeaux and Burgundy to satisfy the most demanding drinker, and plenty more besides. A must-have list – and if you can't make up your mind they do excellent mixed cases.*

Laymont & Shaw

The Old Chapel, Millpool, Truro, Cornwall TR1 1EX (01872) 270545

fax (01872) 223005 e-mail info@laymont-shaw.co.uk

website www.laymont-shaw.co.uk hours Mon–Fri 9–5 cards Maestro, MasterCard, Visa discounts £5 per case if wines collected, also £1 per case for 2 cases, £2 for 3–5, £3 for 6 or more delivery Free UK mainland minimum order 1 mixed case. C G M T

✪ *Excellent, knowledgeable list that specializes in Spain, with something from just about every region.*

Laytons

See Jeroboams.

Lea & Sandeman

170 Fulham Road, London SW10 9PR (020) 7244 0522 fax (020) 7244 0533

• 211 Kensington Church Street, London W8 7LX (020) 7221 1982

• 51 High Street, Barnes, London SW13 9LN (020) 8878 8643 e-mail info@leaandsandeman.co.uk

website www.londonfinewine.co.uk hours Mon–Sat 10–8 cards AmEx, Maestro, MasterCard, Visa

discounts 5–15% by case, other discounts on 10 cases or more delivery £5 for less than 1 case; free 1 case or more London, and to UK mainland south of Perth on orders over £250 en primeur Bordeaux, Burgundy, Italy. C G M T

✪ *Burgundy and Italy take precedence here, and there's a succession of excellent names, chosen with great care. Bordeaux has wines at all price levels, and there are short but fascinating ranges from the USA, Spain, Australia and New Zealand.*

Liberty Wines

mail order Unit D18, New Covent Garden Food Market, London SW8 5LL (020) 7720 5350
fax (020) 7720 6158   website www.libertywine.co.uk   e-mail info@libertywine.co.uk   hours Mon–Fri 9–5.30
cards Maestro, MasterCard, Visa   delivery Free to mainland UK   minimum order 1 mixed case.   M
✪ *Italy rules, with superb wines from pretty well all the best producers. Liberty are the UK agents for most of their producers, so if you're interested in Italian wines, this should be your first port of call. Also top names from Australia and elsewhere.*

Linlithgow Wines

Crossford, Station Road, Linlithgow, West Lothian EH49 6BW   tel & fax (01506) 848821
e-mail jrobmcd@aol.com   hours Mon–Fri 9–5.30 (please phone first)   cards none: cash, cheque or bank transfer only
delivery Free locally; elsewhere in UK £6.50 for 1 case, £4.75 per case for 2 or more. G M T
✪ *Specialist in the south of France – Languedoc, southern Rhône and Provence – with lots around £5–7; prices rarely exceed £20.*

O W Loeb & Co

3 Archie Street, off Tanner Street, London SE1 3JT (020) 7234 0385
fax (020) 7357 0440   e-mail finewine@owloeb.com   website www.owloeb.com
hours Mon–Fri 8.30–5.30   cards Maestro, MasterCard, Visa   discounts 3 cases and above   delivery Free 3 cases or more and on orders over £250   minimum order 1 case   en primeur Burgundy, Bordeaux, Rhône, Germany (Mosel).
C M T
✪ *Burgundy, the Rhône, Loire and Germany stand out, with top producers galore. Then there are Loeb's new discoveries from Spain and the New World, especially New Zealand and South Africa.*

Maison du Vin

Moor Hill, Hawkhurst, Kent TN18 4PF (01580) 753487
fax (01580) 755627   e-mail kvgriffin@aol.com   website www.maison-du-vin.co.uk   hours Mon 10–4, Tue and Thu 10–8, Wed and Fri 10–5, Sat 10–6   cards Access, AmEx, Maestro, MasterCard, Visa   delivery Free locally; UK mainland at cost   en primeur Bordeaux. C G M T
✪ *As the name suggests, the focus is on French wines, at prices from about £6 upwards. There's a monthly themed 'wine school' or you can book personal tutored tastings.*

Majestic

(see also Wine and Beer World)

head office Majestic House, Otterspool Way, Watford, Herts WD25 8WW (01923) 298200
fax (01923) 819105; 136 stores nationwide e-mail info@majestic.co.uk website www.majestic.co.uk
hours Mon–Fri 10–8, Sat 9–7, Sun 10–5 (may vary) cards AmEx, Diners, Maestro, MasterCard, Visa
delivery Free UK mainland minimum order 1 mixed case (12 bottles) en primeur Bordeaux, Port. G M T
✪ *One of the best places to buy Champagne, with a good range and good discounts for buying in quantity. Loads of interesting and reasonably priced stuff, especially from France and the New World.*

Marks & Spencer

head office Waterside House, 35 North Wharf Road, London W2 1NW (020) 7935 4422
fax (020) 7487 2679; 500 licensed stores website www.marksandspencer.com hours Variable
discounts Variable, Wine of the Month, buy any 6 and save 10% in selected stores. M T
✪ *M&S works with top producers around the world to create its impressive list of own-label wines.*

Martinez Wines

35 The Grove, Ilkley, Leeds, West Yorkshire LS29 9NJ (01943) 600000
fax 0870 922 3940 e-mail julian@martinez.co.uk website www.martinez.co.uk
hours Sun 12–6, Mon–Wed 10–8, Thurs–Fri 10–9, Sat 9.30–6 cards AmEx, Maestro, MasterCard, Visa
discounts 5% on 6 bottles or more, 10% off orders over £150 delivery Free local delivery, otherwise £11 per case
mainland UK en primeur Bordeaux, Burgundy. C G M T
✪ *Carefully chosen selection – Alsace and Beaujolais look spot-on, as do Bordeaux, Burgundy and Rhône, so I would trust their selection from other regions.*

Millésima

87 Quai de Paludate, BP 89, 33038 Bordeaux Cedex, France (00 33) 5 57 80 88 08
fax (00 33) 5 57 80 88 19 Freephone 0800 917 0352 website www.millesima.com hours Mon–Fri 8–5.30
cards AmEx, Diners, Maestro, MasterCard, Visa delivery For bottled wines, free to single UK addresses for orders
exceeding £500. Otherwise, a charge of £20 will be applied. For en primeur wines, free to single UK addresses.
en primeur Bordeaux, Burgundy, Rhône. C M T
✪ *Wine comes direct from the châteaux to Millésima's cellars, where 3 million bottles are stored. A sprinkling of established names from other French regions.*

Montrachet

mail order 59 Kennington Road, London SE1 7PZ (020) 7928 1990
fax (020) 7928 3415 e-mail andy@montrachetwine.com website www.montrachetwine.com hours (Office and mail order) Mon–Fri 8.30–5.30 cards Maestro, MasterCard, Visa delivery England and Wales £12 including VAT, free for 3 or more cases; Scotland ring for details minimum order 1 unmixed case en primeur Bordeaux, Burgundy. M T
✪ *Impressive Burgundies are the main attraction here, but there are also some very good Rhônes, and Bordeaux is excellent at all price levels.*

Moreno Wines

11 Marylands Road, London W9 2DU (020) 7286 0678
fax (020) 7286 0513 e-mail merchant@moreno-wines.co.uk website www.morenowinedirect.co.uk
hours Mon–Fri 4–9, Sat 12–9 cards AmEx, Maestro, MasterCard, Visa discounts 10% 2 or more cases
delivery Free locally, 3 or more cases within UK also free, otherwise £7.50. M T
✪ *Specialist in Spanish wines, some fine and rare, with prices to match, but plenty of everyday drinking too.*

Moriarty Vintners

Unit 3, Penarth Road Retail Park, Penarth Road, Cardiff CF11 8TW (02920) 705572
fax (02920) 488300 e-mail david@moriarty-vintners.co.uk website www.moriarty-vintners.co.uk
hours Mon–Thurs 10–6, Fri–Sat 10–8, Sun 12–5 discounts 15% off mixed case delivery free locally, nationwide at cost en primeur Italy, Port, Rhône. C G M T
✪ *Concentrates on exciting gems from small producers. Italy is strong and other regions with good coverage include the Languedoc, Bordeaux, Australia and Spain.*

Wm Morrison Supermarkets

head office Hilmore House, Gain Lane, Bradford, West Yorkshire BD3 7DL 0845 611 5000
fax 0845 611 6801 customer service 0845 611 6111; 368 licensed branches website www.morrisons.co.uk
hours Variable, generally Mon–Sat 8–8, Sun 10–4 cards Amex, Delta, Maestro, MasterCard, Solo, Style, Visa Electron. G T
✪ *Inexpensive, often tasty wines, with masses below £5. But if you're prepared to trade up a little there's some really good stuff here. A handful of clarets, too.*

The following services are available where indicated: C = cellarage **G** = glass hire/loan **M** = mail/online order **T** = tastings and talks

James Nicholson

7/9 Killyleagh Street, Crossgar, Co. Down, Northern Ireland BT30 9DQ (028) 4483 0091
fax (028) 4483 0028 e-mail shop@jnwine.com website www.jnwine.com hours Mon–Sat 10–7
cards Maestro, MasterCard, Visa discounts 10% mixed case delivery Free (1 case or more) in Eire and Northern
Ireland; UK mainland £7.95, 2 cases £10.95 en primeur Bordeaux, Burgundy, California, Rioja, Rhône. C G M T
✪ *Well-chosen list mainly from small, committed growers around the world. Bordeaux, Rhône and southern France are slightly ahead of the field, there's a good selection of Burgundy and some excellent drinking from Germany and Spain.*

Nickolls & Perks

37 Lower High Street, Stourbridge, West Midlands DY8 1TA (01384) 394518
fax (01384) 440786 e-mail sales@nickollsandperks.co.uk website www.nickollsandperks.co.uk
hours Tues–Fri 10.30–5.30, Sat 10.30–5 cards Maestro, MasterCard, Visa discounts negotiable per case
delivery £10 per consignment en primeur Bordeaux, Champagne, Port. C G M T
✪ *Established in 1797, Nickolls & Perks have a wide-ranging list – and a terrific website – covering most areas. Their strength is France. Advice is available to clients wishing to develop their cellars or invest in wine.*

Nidderdale Fine Wines

2a High Street, Pateley Bridge, North Yorkshire HG3 5AW (01423) 711703
e-mail info@southaustralianwines.com website www.southaustralianwines.com hours Every day 10–6
cards Maestro, MasterCard, Visa discounts 5% case discount on shop purchases delivery £5 per case in England,
Wales and southern Scotland; rest of UK £25 per case. Single bottle delivery negotiable. G T
✪ *Specialist in South Australia, with 400 wines broken down into regions. Also 350 or so wines from other parts of Australia and the rest of the world. Look out for online offers and winemaker dinners.*

Noble Rot Wine Warehouses

18 Market Street, Bromsgrove, Worcestershire, B61 8JZ (01527) 575606
fax (01527) 833133 e-mail info@noble-rot.co.uk website www.noble-rot.co.uk
hours Mon–Fri 10–7, Sat 9.30–6.30 cards Maestro, MasterCard, Visa discounts Various
delivery Free within 10-mile radius. G T
✪ *Great for current drinking, mostly at £4 to £15 a bottle. Australia, Italy, France and Spain feature strongly in a frequently changing list of more than 400 wines.*

The Nobody Inn

Doddiscombsleigh, Nr Exeter, Devon EX6 7PS (01647) 252394

fax (01647) 252978   e-mail info@nobodyinn.co.uk   website www.nobodyinn.co.uk

hours Mon–Sun 12–3 & 6–11 (summer)   cards AmEx, Maestro, MasterCard, Visa   discounts 5% per case   delivery £7.99 for 1 case, free over £150.   G M T

• The Nobody Wine Company (01647) 252394   fax (01647) 252978   e-mail sales@thenobodywinecompany.co.uk   website www.thenobodywinecompany.co.uk   hours 24-hr ordering service   delivery Free for orders over £150.

✪ *The sixteenth-century Nobody Inn has an extraordinary list of more than 700 wines. Australia rules, but there's something exciting from just about everywhere, including marvellous sweet wines. The Wine Company is a mail-order venture for wines mostly priced at £5–10.*

Oddbins

head office 31–33 Weir Road, London SW19 8UG (020) 8944 4400

fax (020) 8944 4411   mail order Oddbins Direct 0800 328 2323   fax 0800 328 3848; 210 shops nationwide   website www.oddbins.com   hours Ask local branch for details   cards AmEx, Maestro, MasterCard, Visa   discounts 6 for 5 on Champagne or sparkling wine; 10% off 6 bottles or 20% off 12 bottles of table wine, excluding fine wine; regular general promotions   delivery (Stores) free locally for orders over £100 en primeur Bordeaux.   G M T

• Calais store Cité Europe, 139 Rue de Douvres, 62901, Coquelles Cedex, France (0033) 3 21 82 07 32   fax (0033) 3 21 82 05 83   pre-order www.oddbins.com/storefinder/calais.asp

✪ *New World meets the classic regions of Europe: extensive Aussie selection, well-chosen Chileans, Argentinians and South Africans sit alongside good stuff from all over France, Spain and Italy. Always a good choice of fizz.*

The Oxford Wine Company

The Wine Warehouse, Witney Road, Standlake, Oxon OX29 7PR (01865) 301144

fax (01865) 301155   e-mail info@oxfordwine.co.uk   website www.oxfordwine.co.uk

hours Mon–Sat 9–7, Sun 11–4   cards AmEx, Diners, Maestro, MasterCard, Visa   discounts 5% discount on a case of 12, no minimum order   delivery Free locally; national delivery £9.99 for any amount   en primeur Bordeaux.   G M T

✪ *A good selection from the classic regions and the New World, from bargain basement prices to expensive fine wines. Easy-to-use website. They also organize tastings and other events.*

OZ WINES

mail order Freepost Lon 17656, London SW18 5BR, 0845 450 1261

fax (020) 8870 8839 e-mail sales@ozwines.co.uk website www.ozwines.co.uk hours Mon–Fri 9.30–7

cards Access, Diners, Maestro, MasterCard, Visa delivery Free minimum order 1 mixed case. M T

✪ *Australian wines made by small wineries and real people – wines with the kind of thrilling flavours that Australians do better than anyone else.*

Penistone Court Wine Cellars

The Railway Station, Penistone, Sheffield, South Yorkshire S36 6HP (01226) 766037

fax (01226) 767310 e-mail chris@pcwine.plus.com website www.pcwine.co.uk hours Tues–Fri 10–6, Sat 10–3

cards Maestro, MasterCard, Visa delivery Free locally, rest of UK mainland charged at cost 1 case or more

minimum order 1 case. G M

✪ *A well-balanced list, with something from just about everywhere, mostly from familiar names. Tasty drinking from all over France, plus a good range from Italy, Austria, Spain, Chile, the USA, New Zealand and Australia.*

Philglas & Swiggot

21 Northcote Road, Battersea, London SW11 1NG (020) 7924 4494 • 64 Hill Rise, Richmond, London TW10 6UB (020) 8332 6031 • 22 New Quebec Street, Marylebone, London W1H 7SB (020) 7402 0002

e-mail info@philglas-swiggot.co.uk website www.philglas-swiggot.co.uk hours (Battersea and Richmond) Mon–Sat 11–7, Sun 12–5; (Marylebone) Mon–Sat 11–7 cards AmEx, Maestro, MasterCard, Visa discounts 5% per case delivery Free 1 case locally. G M

✪ *Excellent selections from Australia, Italy, France and Austria – subtle, interesting wines, not blockbuster brands.*

Christopher Piper Wines

1 Silver Street, Ottery St Mary, Devon EX11 1DB (01404) 814139

fax (01404) 812100 e-mail sales@christopherpiperwines.co.uk website www.christopherpiperwines.co.uk

hours Mon–Fri 8.30–5.30, Sat 9–4.30 cards Maestro, MasterCard, Visa discounts 5% mixed case, 10% 3 or more cases delivery Free for orders over £190, otherwise £7.05 per case minimum order (for mail order) 1 mixed case

en primeur Bordeaux, Burgundy, Rhône. C G M T

✪ *Huge range of well-chosen wines that reflect a sense of place and personality, with lots of information to help you make up your mind.*

Terry Platt Wine Merchants

Council Street West, Llandudno LL30 1ED (01492) 874099

fax (01492) 874788 e-mail info@terryplattwines.co.uk website www.terryplattwines.co.uk

hours Mon–Fri 8.30–5.30 cards Access, Maestro, MasterCard, Visa delivery Free locally and UK mainland 5 cases or more minimum order 1 mixed case. G M T

✪ *A wide-ranging list with a sprinkling of good growers from most regions. New World coverage has increased recently.*

Playford Ros

Middle Park, Thirsk, Yorkshire YO7 3AH (01845) 526777

fax (01845) 526888 e-mail sales@playfordros.com website www.playfordros.com

hours Mon–Fri 8–6 cards MasterCard, Visa discounts negotiable delivery Free Yorkshire, Derbyshire, Durham, Newcastle; elsewhere £10–15 or at courier cost minimum order 1 mixed case en primeur Bordeaux, Burgundy. G M T

✪ *A carefully chosen list, with reassuringly recognizable Burgundy, exceptional Australian and good stuff from other French regions, Chile, Oregon and New Zealand. Plenty at the £6–8 mark.*

Portland Wine Co

16 North Parade, off Norris Road, Sale, Cheshire M33 3JS (0161) 962 8752

fax (0161) 905 1291 • 152a Ashley Road, Hale WA15 9SA (0161) 928 0357 • 82 Chester Road, Macclesfield SK11 8DL (01625) 616147 e-mail enquiries@portlandwine.co.uk website www.portlandwine.co.uk

hours Mon–Sat 10–10, Sun 12–9.30 cards Maestro, MasterCard, Visa discounts 5% 2 cases or more, 10% 5 cases or more delivery Free locally, £15 + VAT per consignment nationwide, no minimum order en primeur Bordeaux. C T

✪ *Spain, Portugal and Burgundy are specialities and there's a promising-looking list of clarets. Consumer-friendly list with something at every price level from around the world.*

Quaff Fine Wine Merchant

139–141 Portland Road, Hove BN3 5QJ (01273) 820320

fax (01273) 820326 e-mail sales@quaffit.com website www.quaffit.com hours Mon–Thurs 10–7, Fri–Sat 10–8, Sun 12–7 cards Access, Maestro, MasterCard, Visa discounts 10% mixed case delivery Next working day nationwide, charge depends on order value. C G M T

✪ *Extensive and keenly-priced list organized by grape variety rather than country.*

Raeburn Fine Wines

21–23 Comely Bank Road, Edinburgh EH4 1DS (0131) 343 1159

fax (0131) 332 5166 e-mail sales@raeburnfinewines.com website www.raeburnfinewines.com

hours Mon–Sat 9.30–6, Sun 12.30–1 cards AmEx, Maestro, MasterCard, Visa discounts 5% unsplit case, 2.5% mixed

delivery Free local area 1 or more cases (usually); elsewhere at cost en primeur Australia, Bordeaux, Burgundy, California, Germany, Italy, Languedoc-Roussillon, Loire, New Zealand, Rhône. G M T

✪ *Carefully-chosen list, mainly from small growers. Burgundy and Loire are specialities, with Italy, Austria and northern Spain close behind.*

Real Wine Co.

1 Cannon Meadow, Bull Lane, Gerrards Cross, Buckinghamshire SL9 8RE (01753) 885619

e-mail mark@therealwineco.co.uk website www.therealwineco.co.uk cards Delta, Maestro, Mastercard, Visa

delivery Up to 2 cases £5, free for 3 or more cases to single address; free to postcodes SL9 and HP9 irrespective of number of cases minimum order 1 mixed case

✪ *Owner Mark Hughes has based his list entirely on his personal taste – check it out and see if you agree with him.*

Reid Wines

The Mill, Marsh Lane, Hallatrow, Nr Bristol BS39 6EB (01761) 452645

fax (01761) 453642 e-mail reidwines@aol.com hours Mon–Fri 9–5.30 cards Access, Maestro, MasterCard, Visa (3% charge) delivery Free within 25 miles of Hallatrow (Bristol), and in central London for orders over 2 cases en primeur Claret. C G M T

✪ *A mix of great old wines, some old duds and splendid current stuff. Italy, USA, Australia, port and Madeira look tremendous.*

Richardson & Sons

26a Lowther Street, Whitehaven, Cumbria CA28 7DG

fax/tel (01946) 65334 e-mail mailwines@tiscali.co.uk hours Mon–Sat 10–5.30 cards AmEx, Delta, Maestro, MasterCard, Visa delivery Free locally M T

✪ *Focused on reds from Australia, Bordeaux and Burgundy, with a preference for small producers. Join their mailing list to get regular updates.*

Howard Ripley

25 Dingwall Road, London SW18 3AZ (020) 8877 3065
fax (020) 8877 0029 e-mail info@howardripley.com website www.howardripley.com
hours Mon–Fri 9–6, Sat 9–1 cards Maestro, MasterCard, Visa delivery Minimum charge £10.50 + VAT, free UK mainland on orders over £500 ex-VAT minimum order 1 case en primeur Burgundy, Germany. C M T
✪ A must-have list for serious Burgundy lovers; expensive but not excessive. The German range is also excellent.

Roberson

348 Kensington High Street, London W14 8NS (020) 7371 2121
fax (020) 7371 4010 e-mail retail@roberson.co.uk website www.robersonwinemerchant.co.uk
hours Mon–Sat 10–8 cards Access, AmEx, Diners, Maestro, MasterCard, Visa discounts mail order 5% on champagne and spirits, 10% or wine cases delivery Free delivery within London, otherwise £15 per case en primeur Bordeaux, Port. C G M T
✪ Fine and rare wines, sold by the bottle. All of France is excellent; so is Italy and port.

The RSJ Wine Company

33 Coin Street, London SE1 9NR (020) 7928 4554
fax (020) 7928 9768 e-mail tom.king@rsj.uk.com website www.rsj.uk.com
hours Mon–Fri 9–6, answering machine at other times cards AmEx, Maestro, MasterCard, Visa delivery Free central London, minimum 1 case; England and Wales (per case), £14.10 1 case, £10.25 2 cases or more. G M T
✪ A roll-call of great Loire names, and some good Bordeaux.

Safeway

Now owned by Wm Morrison plc (see page 176)

Sainsbury's

head office 33 Holborn, London EC1N 2HT (020) 7695 6000
customer service 0800 636262; 780 stores website www. sainsburyswine.co.uk – click on Wines to your door for exciting and exclusive offers hours Variable, some 24 hrs, locals generally Mon–Sat 7–11, Sun 10 or 11–4
cards AmEx, Maestro, MasterCard, Visa discounts 5% for 6 bottles or more G M T
• mail order 0800 917 4092 fax 0800 917 4095

- Calais store Sainsbury's, Centre Commercial Auchan, Route de Boulogne, 62100 Calais, France (0033) 3 21 82 38 48 fax (0033) 3 21 36 01 91 preorder www.sainsburys.co.uk/calais
- ✪ *A collection to cater for bargain hunters as well as lovers of good-value wine higher up the scale. They've expanded their Taste the Difference range and got some top producers on board.*

Savage Selection

The Ox House, Market Place, Northleach, Cheltenham, Glos GL54 3EG (01451) 860896
fax (01451) 860996 • The Ox House Shop and Wine Bar at same address (01451) 860680
e-mail wine@savageselection.co.uk website www.savageselection.co.uk hours Office: Mon–Fri 9–6; shop: Tue–Wed 10–7.30, Thur–Fri 10–10, Sat 10–4 cards Maestro, MasterCard, Visa delivery Free locally for orders over £100; elsewhere on UK mainland free for orders over £250: otherwise £11.75 per consignment en primeur Bordeaux. C G M T
✪ *Owner Mark Savage seeks out new and interesting wines from Italy, Spain, Germany and Austria, as well as from Hungary, Greece and Idaho.*

Seckford Wines

Dock Lane, Melton, Suffolk IP12 1PE (01394) 446622
fax (01394) 446633 e-mail sales@seckfordwines.co.uk website www.seckfordwines.co.uk
cards Maestro, MasterCard, Visa delivery £11.75 inc VAT per consignment, UK mainland; elsewhere at cost
minimum order 1 mixed case en primeur Bordeaux, Burgundy. C M
✪ *Bordeaux, Burgundy and the Rhône are the stars of this list, with some excellent older vintages. Serious stuff from Italy, Spain and Austria, too.*

Somerfield

head office Somerfield House, Whitchurch Lane, Bristol BS14 0TJ (0117) 935 9359
fax (0117) 935 6669; 940 Somerfield stores website www.somerfield.co.uk
hours Mon–Sat 8–8, Sun 10–4 cards Maestro, MasterCard, Visa discounts 5% off 6 bottles
delivery Free local delivery for orders over £25 in selected stores.
✪ *Wines from all over, ranging from bargain prices to the £25 mark. Lots of choice on New World wines.*

Sommelier Wine Co.

23 St George's Esplanade, St Peter Port, Guernsey, Channel Islands, GY1 2BG (01481) 721677
fax (01481) 716818 hours Mon–Sat 9.15–5.30, except Fri 9.15–6 cards Maestro, MasterCard, Visa
discounts 5% 1 case or more delivery Free locally 1 mixed case. Customs legislation means that the shipping of wine to the UK mainland is restricted. G T
✪ *An excellent list, with interesting, unusual wines. A big selection of top-notch Australia, Italy, Loire, Beaujolais, Burgundy, Bordeaux, the Rhône, Spain and South Africa.*

Frank Stainton Wines

3 Berry's Yard, Finkle Street, Kendal, Cumbria LA9 4AB (01539) 731886 fax (01539) 730396
e-mail admin@stainton-wines.co.uk website www.stainton-wines.co.uk hours Mon–Fri 9–5.30, Sat 9–4.30
cards Maestro, MasterCard, Visa discounts 5% mixed case delivery Free Cumbria and North Lancashire; elsewhere (per case) £13 1 case, more than 1 case variable. G M T
✪ *The list includes some great Bordeaux, interesting Burgundy, and leading names from Italy and Chile.*

Stevens Garnier

47 West Way, Botley, Oxford OX2 0JF (01865) 263303
fax (01865) 791594 e-mail shop@stevensgarnier.co.uk hours Mon–Thur 10–6, Fri 10–7, Sat 9.30–5.30
cards AmEx, Maestro, MasterCard, Visa, Solo discounts 5% on a mixed case delivery Free locally; 'competitive rates' elsewhere. G M T
✪ *Regional France is a strength: this is one of the few places in the UK you can buy wine from Savoie. Likewise, there are interesting choices from Portugal, Australia, Chile and Canada.*

Stone, Vine & Sun

No. 13 Humphrey Farms, Hazeley Road, Twyford, Winchester SO21 1QA (01962) 712351
fax (01962) 717545 e-mail sales@stonevine.co.uk website www.stonevine.co.uk hours Mon–Fri 9–6, Sat 9.30–4
cards Access, Maestro, MasterCard, Visa discounts 5% on an unmixed case delivery £4.50 per case. Prices vary for Scottish Highlands and islands and Northern Ireland. Free delivery for orders over £250 G M T
✪ *Lovely list marked by enthusiasm and passion for the subject. Lots of interesting stuff from France, but also from Germany, South Africa, New Zealand and elsewhere.*

Sunday Times Wine Club

New Aquitaine House, Exeter Way, Theale, Reading, Berks RG7 4PL

order line 0870 220 0020 fax 0870 220 0030 e-mail orders@sundaytimeswineclub.co.uk
website www.sundaytimeswineclub.co.uk hours 24-hr answering machine cards AmEx, Diners, Maestro, MasterCard, Visa delivery £5.99 per order en primeur Australia, Bordeaux, Burgundy, Rhône. C M T

✪ *Essentially the same as Laithwaites (see page 172), though the special offers come round at different times. The membership fee is £10 per annum. The club runs tours and tasting events for its members.*

T & W Wines

5 Station Way, Brandon, Suffolk IP27 0BH (01842) 814414

fax (01842) 819967 e-mail contact@tw-wines.com website www.tw-wines.com hours Mon–Fri 9.30–5.30, occasional Sat 9.30–1 cards AmEx, MasterCard, Visa delivery (most areas) 7–23 bottles £14.95 + VAT, 2 or more cases free en primeur Burgundy. C G M T

✪ *A good list, particularly if you're looking for Burgundy, Rhône, Alsace or the Loire, but prices are not especially low.*

Tanners

26 Wyle Cop, Shrewsbury, Shropshire SY1 1XD (01743) 234500 fax (01743) 234501
• 4 St Peter's Square, Hereford HR1 2PG (01432) 272044 fax (01432) 263316
• 36 High Street, Bridgnorth WV16 4DB (01746) 763148 fax (01746) 769798
• Severn Farm Enterprise Park, Welshpool SY21 7DF (01938) 552542 fax (01938) 556565
e-mail sales@tanners-wines.co.uk website www.tanners-wines.co.uk hours Shrewsbury Mon–Sat 9–6, branches 9–5.30 cards AmEx, Maestro, MasterCard, Visa discounts 5% 1 mixed case, 7.5% 5 mixed cases (cash & collection); 2.5% for 3 mixed cases, 5% for 5, 7.5% for 10 mail order delivery Free 1 mixed case over £90, otherwise £7.50 minimum order £25 en primeur Bordeaux, Burgundy, Rhône, Germany, Port. C G M T

✪ *There are lots of lovely Rhônes; Bordeaux, Burgundy and Germany are terrific; there are even a couple of wines from Switzerland, Greece and Lebanon. Well-chosen own-label fortified wines.*

Tesco

head office Tesco House, PO Box 18, Delamare Road, Cheshunt EN8 9SL (01992) 632222
fax (01992) 630794 customer service 0800 505555; 916 licensed branches e-mail customer.services@tesco.co.uk
website www.tesco.com hours Variable cards Maestro, MasterCard, Visa discount 5% on 6 bottles or more G M T
• calais store Tesco Vin Plus, Cité Europe, 122 Boulevard du Kent, 62231 Coquelles, France (0033) 3 21 46 02 70

website www.tesco.com/vinplus; www.tesco-france.com hours Mon–Sat 8.30–10pm
✪ *You can buy premium wines at around £20, bargain basement bottles or anything in between. Tesco.com offers an even greater selection of wines by the case.*

Thresher Group: Thresher Wine Shops and Wine Rack

head office Enjoyment Hall, Bessemer Road, Welwyn Garden City, Herts AL7 1BL (01707) 387200
fax (01707) 387350 website www.threshergroup.com; 840 Thresher Wine Shops, 266 Wine Rack stores
hours Mon–Sat 10–10 (some 10.30), Sun 11–10, Scotland 12.30–10.30 cards Maestro, MasterCard, Visa
delivery Free locally, some branches. G T
✪ *Australia and France take the leading roles, with strong support from Spain, New Zealand and South Africa. The popular 3 for 2 deal means you'll get some real bargains if you buy any 3 bottles – but some single bottle prices are on the high side.*

Turville Valley Wines

The Firs, Potter Row, Great Missenden, Bucks HP16 9LT (01494) 868818
fax (01494) 868832 e-mail chris@turville-valley-wines.com website www.turville-valley-wines.com
hours Mon–Fri 9–5.30 cards None delivery By arrangement minimum order £300/12 bottles. C M
✪ *Serious wines for serious spenders. The Bordeaux is all classic, mostly mature, and there are top names too from Spain, Italy, the Rhône, California and Australia.*

Valvona & Crolla

19 Elm Row, Edinburgh EH7 4AA (0131) 556 6066
fax (0131) 556 1668 e-mail wine@valvonacrolla.co.uk website www.valvonacrolla.com
hours Shop: Mon–Sat 8–6.30, Sun 10.30–5, Caffe bar: Mon–Sat 8–6, Sun 10.30–4.30
cards AmEx, Maestro, MasterCard, Visa discounts 7% 1–3 cases, 10% 4 or more delivery Free on orders over £150,
otherwise £9; Saturdays free on orders over £200, otherwise £15. G M T
✪ *A fabulous selection of wines from every region of Italy, including Sicily and Sardinia.*

Villeneuve Wines

1 Venlaw Court, Peebles, Scotland EH45 8AE (01721) 722500 fax (01721) 729922
• 82 High Street, Haddington EH41 3ET (01620) 822224
• 49A Broughton Street, Edinburgh EH1 3RJ (0131) 558 8441
e-mail wines@villeneuvewines.com website www.villeneuvewines.com hours (Peebles) Mon–Sat 9–8, Sun

12.30–5.30; (Haddington) Mon–Sat 9–7; (Edinburgh) Mon–Wed 12.30–10, Thurs 10–10, Fri–Sat 9–10, Sun 12.30–10
cards AmEx, Maestro, MasterCard, Visa discounts 5% per case delivery Free locally, £8.50 per case elsewhere. G M T
✪ *Italy, California, Australia and New Zealand are all marvellous here. Spain is clearly an enthusiasm, too.*

Vinceremos

74 Kirkgate, Leeds LS2 7DJ 0800 107 3068
fax (0113) 288 4566 e-mail info@vinceremos.co.uk website www.vinceremos.co.uk hours Mon–Fri 8.30–5.30
cards AmEx, Delta, Maestro, MasterCard, Visa discounts 5% on 5 cases or over, 10% on 10 cases or over
delivery Free 5 cases or more minimum order 1 mixed case M
✪ *Organic specialist, with a wide-ranging list of wines.*

Vin du Van

mail order Colthups, The Street, Appledore, Kent TN26 2BX (01233) 758727 fax (01233) 758389
hours Mon–Fri 9–5 cards Delta, Maestro, MasterCard, Visa delivery Free locally; elsewhere £5.95 for first case, further
cases free. Highlands and islands, ask for quote minimum order 1 mixed case. M
✪ *Extensive, wonderfully quirky, star-studded Australian list.*

Vintage Roots

Farley Farms, Reading Road, Arborfield, Berkshire, RG2 9HT (0118) 976 1999
fax (0118) 976 1998 hours Mon–Fri 8.30–5.30, Saturdays in December e-mail info@vintageroots.co.uk
website www.vintageroots.co.uk cards Delta, Maestro, MasterCard, Visa discounts 5% on 5 cases or over
delivery £6.95 for any delivery under 5 cases; more than 6 cases is free. Some local deliveries free. Cases can be mixed.
Overnight is an extra £2.50 per case. G M T
✪ *Everything on this list is organic and/or biodynamic, from Champagne and other fizz to beer and cider. Chile, France,
Spain and Italy look good.*

Virgin Wines

mail order The Loft, St James' Mill, Whitefriars, Norwich NR3 1TN 0870 164 9593
fax (01603) 619277 e-mail help@virginwines.com website www.virginwines.com
hours (office) Mon–Fri 8.30–6.30, Sat 10–4, Internet 24 hrs cards AmEx, Maestro, MasterCard, Visa
discounts regular special offers delivery £5.99 per order for all UK deliveries minimum order 1 case. M T
✪ *Online retailer with reasonably priced wines from all over the world. Well-balanced mixed cases, or you can mix your own.*

Waitrose

head office Doncastle Road, Southern Industrial Area, Bracknell, Berkshire RG12 8YA
customer service 0800 188884, 185 licensed stores e-mail customerservice@waitrose.co.uk
website www.waitrose.com/wines hours Mon–Sat 8.30–7, 8 or 9, Sun 10–4 or 11–5 cards AmEx, Delta, Maestro,
MasterCard, Partnership Card, Visa discounts Regular monthly promotions, 5% off for 6 bottles or more
home delivery Available through www.waitrosedeliver.co.uk and www.ocado.com and Waitrose Wine Direct (below)
en primeur Bordeaux and Burgundy available through Waitrose Wine Direct G T
• waitrose wine direct order online at www.waitrose.com/wines or 0800 188881
e-mail wineadvisor@johnlewis.com discounts Vary monthly on featured cases; branch promotions are matched. All
cases include a 5% discount to match branch offer. delivery Free for orders of £100 or more throughout UK mainland,
Northern Ireland and Isle of Wight, otherwise £3.95 per addressee. Named day delivery – £6.95 per addressee (order by
3pm for next working day). Next day delivery pre-10.30am – £9.95 per addressee (order by 3pm for next working day).
✪ *Ahead of the other supermarkets in quality, value and imagination. Still lots of tasty stuff under £5.*

Waterloo Wine Co

office and warehouse 6 Vine Yard, London SE1 1QL
shop 59–61 Lant Street, London SE1 1QL (020) 7403 7967 fax (020) 7357 6976 e-mail sales@waterloowine.co.uk
website www.waterloowine.co.uk hours Mon–Fri 11–7.30, Sat 10–5 cards AmEx, Maestro, MasterCard, Visa delivery
Free 5 cases in central London (otherwise £5); elsewhere, 1 case £12, 2 cases £7.50 each. G T
✪ *Quirky, personal list, strong in the Loire and New Zealand.*

Whitesides of Clitheroe

Shawbridge Street, Clitheroe, Lancs BB7 1NA (01200) 422281
fax (01200) 427129 e-mail whitesides.wine@btconnect.com hours Mon–Fri 9–5.30, Sat 10–4
cards Maestro, MasterCard, Visa discounts 5% per case delivery Free locally, elsewhere at cost. G M T
✪ *Half New World, half Europe, with some interesting selections hidden among the sub-£5 stuff.*

Wimbledon Wine Cellar

1 Gladstone Road, Wimbledon, London SW19 1QU (020) 8540 9979 fax (020) 8540 9399
• 84 Chiswick High Road, London W4 1SY (020) 8994 7989 fax (020) 8994 3683
• 4 The Boulevard, Imperial Wharf, Chelsea, London SW6 2UB (020) 7736 2191 e-mail enquiries@
wimbledonwinecellar.com, chiswick@wimbledonwinecellar.com or chelsea@wimbledonwinecellar.com

website www.wimbledonwinecellar.com hours Mon–Sat 10–9, Sun 11–7 (all stores) cards AmEx, Maestro, MasterCard, Visa discounts 10% off 1 case (with a few exceptions), 20% off case of Champagne delivery Free local delivery. Courier charges elsewhere en primeur Burgundy, Bordeaux, Tuscany, Rhône. C G M T

☼ *Top names from Italy, Burgundy, Bordeaux, Rhône, Loire – and some of the best of the New World.*

Wine & Beer World (Majestic)
head office Majestic House, Otterspool Way, Watford, Herts WD25 8WW (01923) 298200
fax (01923) 819105 e-mail info@wineandbeer.co.uk website www.wineandbeer.co.uk
• Rue du Judée, Zone Marcel Doret, Calais 62100, France (0033) 3 21 97 63 00
• Centre Commercial Carrefour, Quai L'Entrepôt, Cherbourg 50100, France (0033) 2 33 22 23 22
• Unit 3A, Zone La Française, Coquelles 62331, France (0033) 3 21 82 93 64
pre-order (01923) 298297 hours (Calais) 7 days 8–10 (Cherbourg) Mon–Sat 9–7.30 (Coquelles) 7 days 8–8. Calais and Coquelles open Bank Holidays at the usual times. There is a free ferry crossing from Dover to Calais when your pre-order is over £300. cards Maestro, MasterCard, Visa. T

☼ *The French arm of Majestic, with savings of up to 50% on UK prices. Calais is the largest branch and Coquelles the nearest to the Channel Tunnel terminal. English-speaking staff.*

Winemark
3 Duncrue Place, Belfast BT3 9BU (028) 9074 6274
fax (028) 9074 8022; 71 branches e-mail info@ winemark.com website www.winemark.com hours Branches vary, but in general Mon–Sat 10–10, Sun 12–8 cards Delta, Maestro, MasterCard, Visa discounts 5% on 6–11 bottles, 10% on 12 bottles or more. G M T

☼ *Strong in the New World, with some interesting Australia, New Zealand, Chile and California. Also a shortish but good list of Bordeaux from older vintages.*

Wine Rack
See Thresher Group.

The Wine Society
Gunnels Wood Road, Stevenage, Herts SG1 2BG (01438) 741177
fax (01438) 761167 order line (01438) 740222 e-mail memberservices@thewinesociety.com
website www.thewinesociety.com hours Mon–Fri 8.30–9, Sat 9–5; showroom: Mon–Fri 10–6, Thurs 10–7,

Sat 9.30–5.30 cards Maestro, MasterCard, Visa discounts (per case) £3 per collection delivery Free 1 case or more UK mainland and Northern Ireland. Collection facility at Montreuil, France, at French rates of duty and VAT en primeur Bordeaux, Burgundy, Germany, Port, Rhône.

✪ *An outstanding list from an inspired wine-buying team. Masses of well-chosen affordable wines as well as big names.*

Wine Treasury

mail order 69–71 Bondway, London SW8 1SQ (020) 7793 9999

fax (020) 7793 8080 e-mail bottled@winetreasury.com website www.winetreasury.com hours Mon–Fri 9.30–6 cards Maestro, MasterCard, Visa discounts 10% for unmixed dozens delivery £10 per case, free 2 or more cases over £200, England and Wales; Scotland phone for more details minimum order 1 mixed case. M T

✪ *Excellent choices and top names from California and Italy – but they don't come cheap.*

The Winery

4 Clifton Road, London W9 1SS (020) 7286 6475

fax (020) 7286 2733 e-mail info@thewineryuk.com website www.thewineryuk.com hours Mon–Sat 11–9.30, Sun and public holidays 12–8 cards Maestro, MasterCard, Visa discounts 5% on a mixed case delivery Free locally or for 3 cases or more, otherwise £10 per case. G M T

✪ *Burgundy, Rhône, Italy and California are the specialities, and there's a range of grower Champagnes.*

Wines of Westhorpe

136a Doncaster Road, Mexborough, South Yorkshire S64 0JW (01709) 584863

fax (01709) 584863 e-mail wines@westhorpe.co.uk website www. westhorpe.co.uk hours Mon–Thu 9–8, Fri–Sat 9–6 cards AmEx, Maestro, MasterCard, Visa discounts Variable on 2 dozen or more delivery Free UK mainland (except northern Scotland) minimum order 1 mixed case. M

✪ *An excellent list for devotees of Eastern European wines – especially Hungarian and Romanian – all at reasonable prices.*

Wright Wine Co

The Old Smithy, Raikes Road, Skipton, North Yorkshire BD23 1NP (01756) 700886 (01756) 794175

fax (01756) 798580 e-mail bob@wineandwhisky.co.uk website www.wineandwhisky.co.uk hours Mon–Fri 9–6; Sat 10–5:30; open Sundays in December 10.30–4 cards Maestro, MasterCard, Visa discounts 10% unsplit case, 5% mixed case delivery Free within 30 miles, elsewhere at cost. G

✪ *Equally good in both Old World and New World, with plenty of good stuff at keen prices. Wide choice of half bottles.*

Peter Wylie Fine Wines

Plymtree Manor, Plymtree, Cullompton, Devon EX15 2LE (01884) 277555
fax (01884) 277557 e-mail peter@wylie-fine-wines. demon.co.uk website www.wylie finewines.co.uk
hours Mon–Fri 9–6 cards None discounts Only on unsplit cases delivery Up to 3 cases in London £20, 4 or more cases
at cost. C M
✪ *Fascinating list of very old wines; Bordeaux from throughout the 20th century, ports going back to 1904.*

Yapp Brothers

The Old Brewery, Mere, Wilts BA12 6DY (01747) 860423 fax (01747) 860929
e-mail sales@yapp.co.uk website www.yapp.co.uk hours Mon–Sat 9–6 cards Maestro, MasterCard, Visa
discounts £6 per case on collection delivery £6 one case, 2 or more cases free. C G M T
✪ *Rhône and Loire specialists. They also have some of the hard-to-find wines of Provence, Savoie and Corsica.*

Noel Young Wines

56 High Street, Trumpington, Cambridge CB2 9LS (01223) 844744
fax (01223) 844736 e-mail admin@nywines.co.uk website www.nywines.co.uk
hours Mon–Fri 10–8, Sat 10–7, Sun 12–2 cards AmEx, Maestro, MasterCard, Visa discounts 5% for orders over £500
delivery Free over 12 bottles unless discounted en primeur Australia, Burgundy, Italy, Rhône. G M T
✪ *Fantastic wines from just about everywhere. Australia is a particular passion and there is a great Austrian list, some
terrific Germans, plus beautiful Burgundies, Italians and dessert wines.*

The following services are available where indicated: **C** = cellarage **G** = glass hire/loan **M** = mail/online order **T** = tastings and talks

Who's where

COUNTRYWIDE/ MAIL ORDER ONLY
Adnams
Aldi
ASDA
L'Assemblage
H & H Bancroft Wines
Bibendum Wine
Bordeaux Index
Anthony Byrne
ChateauOnline
Co-op
Devigne Wines
Nick Dobson Wines
Domaine Direct
Fine Wines of New
 Zealand
Roger Harris Wines
Jeroboams
Justerini & Brooks
Laithwaites
Lay & Wheeler
Laytons
Liberty Wines
O W Loeb
Majestic
Marks & Spencer
Millésima
Montrachet
Morrisons
Oddbins
OZ WINES
Real Wine Co
Howard Ripley
Sainsbury's
Somerfield
Stone, Vine & Sun
Sunday Times Wine Club

Tesco
Thresher
Vin du Van
Vintage Roots
Virgin Wines
Waitrose
Wine Rack
The Wine Society
Wine Treasury
Wines of Westhorpe
Peter Wylie Fine Wines
Yapp Brothers
Noel Young Wines

LONDON
Armit
Balls Brothers
Berkmann Wine Cellars
Berry Bros. & Rudd
Budgens
Corney & Barrow
Farr Vintners
Fortnum & Mason
Friarwood
Goedhuis & Co
Green & Blue
Handford Wines
Harvey Nichols
Haynes Hanson & Clark
Jeroboams
Lea & Sandeman
Moreno Wines
Philglas & Swiggot
Roberson
RSJ Wine Company
Waterloo Wine Co
Wimbledon Wine Cellar
The Winery

SOUTH-EAST AND HOME COUNTIES
A&B Vintners
Bacchus Wine
Berry Bros. & Rudd
Budgens
Butlers Wine Cellar
Cape Wine and Food
Les Caves de Pyrene
Flagship Wines
Le Fleming Wines
The Flying Corkscrew
Hedley Wright
Maison du Vin
Quaff Fine Wine
 Merchant
Turville Valley Wines

WEST AND SOUTH-WEST
Averys Wine Merchants
Bennetts Fine Wines
Berkmann Wine Cellars
Great Western Wine
Haynes Hanson & Clark
Hicks & Don
Laymont & Shaw
The Nobody Inn
Christopher Piper Wines
Reid Wines
Savage Selection
Peter Wylie Fine Wines
Yapp Brothers

EAST ANGLIA
Adnams
Budgens
Anthony Byrne

Corney & Barrow
Hicks & Don
Seckford Wines
T & W Wines
Noel Young Wines

MIDLANDS
Bat & Bottle
Connolly's
Croque-en-Bouche
deFINE
Gauntleys
Harvey Nichols
S H Jones
Nickolls & Perks
Noble Rot Wine
 Warehouses
Oxford Wine Co
Portland Wine Co
Stevens Garnier
Tanners

WALES
Ballantynes Wine
 Merchants
Irma Fingal-Rock
Moriarty Vintners
Terry Platt Wine
 Merchants
Tanners

NORTH
Berkmann Wine Cellars
Booths
D Byrne
Great Northern Wine
Halifax Wine Co
Harvey Nichols

Martinez Wines
Nidderdale Fine Wines
Penistone Court Wine
 Cellars
Playford Ros
Richardson & Sons
Frank Stainton Wines
Vinceremos
Whitesides of Clitheroe
Wright Wine Co

SCOTLAND
Berkmann Wine Cellars
Cockburns of Leith
Corney & Barrow
Friarwood
Peter Green & Co
Harvey Nichols
Linlithgow Wines
Raeburn Fine Wines
Valvona & Crolla
Villeneuve Wines

NORTHERN IRELAND
Direct Wine Shipments
James Nicholson
Winemark

CHANNEL ISLANDS
Sommelier Wine Co

FRANCE
Millésima
Oddbins
Sainsbury's
Tesco Vin Plus
Wine & Beer World